To: Jon & Mary Johnson

Freedom is On the other
Side of Forgiveness

8/21/2013

"Cured' is a fascinating Autobiography that epitomizes the essence of the power that one has to truly forgive. Faithfully driven, Carl Ray's life becomes a vehicle that challenges the psyche of man and woman-kind when faced with a terrible injustice.

- Filmmaker Keith A. Beauchamp, "The Untold Story of Emmitt Louis Till."

"The Power in the "Power of Forgiveness" is awesome and redemptive. It is inspiring and motivating to discover the wonders of forgiveness. This is a must read for personal enrichment and growth. Brother Carl Ray has captured the essential element of a fulfilled life: FORGIVENESS."

-Benjamin Jones, St. James Baptist Church – Montgomery, AL

"Carl Ray's long "Journey to Forgiveness" began in 1962 when his father was brutally murdered by a white supremacist in Choctaw County, Ala. Reading his story reveals the true meaning of "The Power of Forgiveness."

– The Richmond Register

"Forgiveness is first and foremost about you and not the individual or individuals who mistreated you. Those who mistreated you didn't spend sleepless nights thinking about what they did to you. They are free of you and moving on with their lives."

-from "Cured"

"Carl Ray's story is undeniably American. It's an honest examination of our nation at its worst and at its best. But ultimately, and most importantly, Carl's story is a story of personal triumph. While he could have easily become an angry, tragic statistic after witnessing his father's murder, Carl instead has become a survivor -- thanks to his ability to forgive. I commend my friend for being transparent about his journey, sharing with the rest of us how mercy and grace turned hate and pain into love."

-David Person, USA Today board of contributors

"Carl Ray tells a story that is chilling in its detail about racially motivated killing in the America of the 1960s. However, this story is inspiring as it points the reader toward the healing power of forgiveness. Carl Ray found a way to forgive the man who murdered his father. It reminds me of the words of Howard Thurman who said "There is no faith without forgiveness." Carl Ray has kept the faith."

-Rev. Marvin McMickle – Antioch Baptist Church
Cleveland, OH

"Years after his father was killed by a white man upset because he wasn't called "sir", Carl turns his pain into a play, wrote this book with a powerful message on forgiveness and finally closes a chapter in his life."

– The Mobile Register

"Carl Ray is one of the world's greatest unsung humanitarians, and has of necessity learned the great truth of the power of forgiveness. This book will prove to be a real treasure."

-Brad Sanders, Comedian, Actor, Producer

CURED

The Power of Forgiveness

Carl Ray with J. Toy Snipes

authorHOUSE®

AuthorHouse™
1663 Liberty Drive
Bloomington, IN 47403
www.authorhouse.com
Phone: 1-800-839-8640

Published by AuthorHouse 9/26/2012

ISBN: 978-1-4670-4462-2 (sc)
ISBN 978-1-4670-4460-8 (e)

Library of Congress Control Number: 2011917870

Any people depicted in stock imagery provided by Thinkstock are models,
and such images are being used for illustrative purposes only.
Certain stock imagery © Thinkstock.

DEDICATIONS

This book is dedicated to the memory of my parents George and Vidella Ray who loved me and my siblings and demanded that we strive to better our lives through education. The rule in our house was, "You are not grown until you get a B.S. Degree."

To the memory of all of my mentors at Tuskegee Institute (University). Without the guidance of this army of angels graduating from college would only have been a dream. Dr. Joseph Fuller, Mrs. Willie McGregor, Mr. Roland Henry, Mr. Guy Trammel, Dr. Eugene Dibble, Mrs. Fannye Harris, Mr. James Harris, Mrs. Larkin, Mrs. Whitehead, Dean Hardwick, Rev. Daniel Wynn, Mr. Lampkin, Mrs. Maude Johnson, Mrs. E. Wright, Mr. Hebert Middlebrooks, Mr. Kermit Todd and Mrs. W. C. Christian.

To my children, Vicki, Lillie, Ejalu, Amelia and Ania. Thanks for loving and supporting me as I struggled constantly in search of my dreams.

ACKNOWLEDGEMENTS

I would like to pay tribute to family and friends that have supported me and my careers. To my loving wife Brenda, who has supported me in every endeavor I have undertaken. Holding the family together as I changed careers from engineer to comedian to motivational speaker to actor to... you are truly an angel sent from God.

To my siblings and their spouses, Elaine (Edward), Lindsey (Fannie), Lemarvin (Barbara) and Louida. Thanks for being great role models.

A special thanks to my friend, fellow comedian and co-writer of this book, J. Toy Snipes; for his time, patience and wisdom in making my dream of writing this book become a reality.

Thanks to my friends who read and edited the book: Carolyn Johnson, Mitz Hayes, Gwen Carr, Gloria Weddington, Shirley Cook, Linda Wells-Hott, Joyce Ruffin-Pace, Carol Pogash, Alberta Martin and my daughter Amelia Ray.

To Tommy and Gail Fulcher, who conceived the idea of my one-man play, giving birth to this journey. Words cannot express my gratitude.

CONTENTS

1

MY ENTRANCE
INTO THE WORLD

Some souls must burn in hell for the torment I experienced in life. Although God appointed angels to guide me through the dark valleys of my life, I wanted someone to pay. Those responsible for thrusting me into a world of endless nightmares, terror and agony, should also suffer on this side of life, before experiencing the wrath of hell and an eternity in damnation.

The morning of September 6, 1962 was beautiful as the sun rose above the treetops along the edge of the cotton field. The sounds of mocking birds chirping and roosters crowing filled the air with beautiful music as I tended my morning chores of feeding the chickens, cows and hogs. Stopping to give my horse Buck a good rub down, I gently explained to her that I was going away to college but would return home for the Christmas break. I talked to all of the farm animals to assure them that they would be alright without me. However, the pigs didn't seem to care about my little going away pep talk. The looks on their faces seemed to say, "Just shut up and give us our corn so we can get back to wallowing in our mud hole." At that time, I had no way of knowing that this would be the last chat with my beloved farm animals. Before the sun had an opportunity to hide itself beyond the west end of the valley, I would be cast into the depths of hell without leaving the surface of the earth; and locked into a nightmare that would last for over forty years.

I was preparing to leave Choctaw County, Alabama where I was born and lived most of my life. Life in Choctaw County, and throughout most of the south was completely segregated. Whites and blacks lived in separate communities. Every area of life was segregated including schools, churches, restaurants, water fountains, and restrooms. Blacks were not allowed the use of public libraries, parks, and swimming pools, even though their tax dollars were used to build and maintain them. School buses were not provided for most black children, resulting in them having to walk several miles to and from school each day.

Blacks lived under an apartheid system which relegated them to second-class citizenship in a black/white society. The majority of blacks lived in rural farm areas with dirt roads and homes without electricity, telephones, toilets, or indoor plumbing. Kerosene lamps provided light, buckets were used to get water from the wells or streams and the toilets (outhouses) were located several yards from the house. Homes were heated with fireplaces and wood burning stoves. These were the conditions under which I began my journey in life.

The first months of my life were touch and go, prompting most of my relatives to come by just to see the tiny baby who probably wouldn't be around very long. My life began on August 30, 1944 in the community of Mt. Olive, just a stone's throw from the flourishing town of Butler, Alabama. Even though there was a major highway running through town, both places seemed somewhat isolated as they sat near the Mississippi border in the southwest corner of the state. That year I was ushered into this world at home with the aid

2

of a midwife as were many other black babies in the county. I became the baby brother to four older siblings, Elanie, Lindsey, Lemarvin, and Louida. Being the last child born to George and Vidella Ray, I was two months premature and weighed less than two pounds. While growing up, I was often reminded by my paternal grandmother, Laura Ann Ray, that the only person that really expected me to live was Momma.

My grandfather, George Ray II, who initially visited shortly after my birth was so sure I wasn't going to survive, he vowed that he would not return to see me unless I lived a month. Even though he only lived about two hundred yards up the road; he kept true to his word. Miraculously, I did survive that first month and as I grew, Granny would often tell me this story and would always end it with a laugh, "Well, you sho' did kick dirt in his face."

Momma just refused to allow me to die. Since I was so small and fragile, she had to make a special bra to carry me next to her bosom. After a couple of visits to the doctor, he informed her that she could probably do more for me than he could ever do. Back in the community, I became a circus side show of sorts because most people had never seen a baby so small.

My second setback in life occurred when I was just eleven months old. While playing with me, two of my siblings accidentally dropped me. Being kids and afraid of the consequences they failed to tell Momma. It wasn't until a few nights later when Momma wasn't able to stop my crying that she walked over a mile with me to the church where Daddy and my brothers and sisters were attending a revival meeting. Momma's concern was justified because after rushing me to the doctor, they discovered my collarbone had been broken. When Momma and Daddy returned home and confronted Lemarvin and Louida, they quickly confessed to their actions.

If staying alive and surviving with two siblings that obviously seemed not to have a need for a little brother wasn't enough, at four years old I woke up one morning and discovered I was completely paralyzed. The right side of my body from my shoulder down to my waist was paralyzed. I had contracted polio, a disease for which there was no cure or prevention. Another medical crisis had visited me and my family. I often wondered how devastated Momma must have felt. Was having a child like myself some type of test that would eventually prepare her for some sort of major crisis in life?

My most vivid memories about the early days of living with polio were the visits to the county health clinic in Butler. Twice a year health officials would round up all of the polio victims in the county and have their parents bring them to the clinic. Even at my young age, I saw no apparent reason for the round-ups except to count bodies. The children in the worst condition were sent a hundred miles away to another clinic in Mobile, Alabama. I would cry because I was afraid I would be torn away from Momma. I thought I would die if I had to be separated from my family even if it was just for a few hours. I would always begin crying before we left home, pleading my case to Momma, telling her how I didn't need to go because I wasn't as sick as those other children. I would look for the kids that appeared to be in worse condition than I was and point them out to convince her that I shouldn't be included with them. Fortunately, I was never chosen to be sent to the clinic in Mobile.

The worst case of polio I ever saw was a young girl whose stricken body was bent over backwards to the point where her head and feet were almost meeting. When the nurses turned her onto her side, she was almost round like the letter

"O." The doctors ordered a specially made pillow that was placed in the arch of her back to support her. I overheard someone refer to her as a freak. Even though I had no idea what that meant, I knew it wasn't anything good.

Frustrated, the doctors and nurses didn't know what to do with us so they gave our parents the best instructions they could on providing therapy to their children at home. Momma would massage my hand, arm and shoulder daily. She would gently place her finger in my hand and encourage me to squeeze it. This procedure went on for about two years. I would become so frustrated because no matter how hard I tried, I could never manage to move a single muscle in my hand or my arm. In tears, I would constantly plead with her to stop. I was convinced that I was never going to be able to use my hand or arm and had accepted the fact that I was a "flicked" kid. I had first heard the word "flicked" from people working at the clinic. "Flicked" was an Ebonics pronunciation for the word, "afflicted" which was used to describe people who suffered from a physical disability.

One day after what seemed like a thousand years of trying, I noticed a slight flinch in my hand and ran to show Momma. She became excited and overjoyed, as if I had climbed Mt. Everest or swam a vast ocean. Her baby was going to be all right! It would be several months later before I could actually grip Momma's finger, but in order to build up and strengthen my hand muscles, she started me on a lifting regiment which consisted of lifting a small pail of sand several times a day. This was really homemade therapy at its best. Instead of a metal brace that many of the white children wore, I had a homemade arm sling made out of flour sackcloth.

As a disabled child, I often missed out on the pleasures of playing childhood games. My days were usually spent watching the other kids running around the yard, wrestling, playing hide and seek and football. I would sit on the porch with the mothers as they quilted, shelled peas, corn, or peeled fruit for canning. Occasionally the mothers would kindly encourage the boys to let me play football with them. Because they were not allowed to tackle me, I would always get to run the length of the entire yard and score. Being good sports, the kids were great actors as they threw themselves on the ground pretending to miss tackling or touching me as I ran past them. But as always, after a few minutes, a frustrated kid would eventually step forward and say to the moms, "Okay, we played with him. Now can he get back on the porch so we can go back to playing rough?" Most of the kids my age would soon be starting school and no way was Polio going to prevent me from joining them.

When I was five years old, I entered Mt. Olive School, a one-room school for first through sixth grade students. The only teacher, Miss. James, lived with us and was much like a family member. Even though I attended almost every day, I didn't know that I wasn't really officially enrolled into school until the school term ended which meant that I didn't get promoted from the first to the second grade as I expected. Momma told me that she sent me to school so I would have kids to play with rather than being home with her all day. At that time her explanation didn't ease the pain of rejection for a five year old mind. In reality, school was more of a baby-sitter or daycare than a place of learning. Whenever I got the urge to go home, I wouldn't hesitate to get up and "hit the road." School was only about a mile from my house and at that time there wasn't much danger of a little boy routinely walking the long country road all by himself. One good thing I can say about school is that it gave me the opportunity to get out of the house and hang out with other kids. It really wasn't like a normal school because almost all of the students were my cousins.

They all treated me differently, because of my disability, during playground activities such as tag, stickball and just plain roughhousing. Since I only had use of my left hand, one of the bigger kids would stand behind me and hold my hands on the stick bat to help me swing at the pitched ball. Whenever I was fortunate enough to strike the ball, I would excitedly run as fast as I could to first base with my right arm swinging freely in the air as my friends cheered me on. I was beaming with joy because I was finally being treated as a normal kid... well almost.

All of that changed the following year when Mt. Olive School closed because of low enrollment and all of the students had to transfer to Butler Public School located in town. Since there was no bus service, we had to walk the entire four miles to school. The lack of public transportation didn't really pose a problem, because very few families in my community owned cars. Getting about on foot was just a part of everyday life.

The second and third grades turned out to be good years because I was known as the little sickly kid and would often receive special attention just as I had when I attended Mt Olive. Because of the lack of any feeling in my hand and arm, I discovered that my classmates enjoyed poking and pinching me. Initially, I didn't like this and refused to allow it to go on until a persistent playmate offered me a nickel if I would allow him to pinch me just once. Before I knew it, I was raking in other kids' money, lunches, and candy just for allowing them to pinch me. I had suddenly become a businessman and had opened my first shop. Eventually, Momma saw the bruises on my arm and became angry with me for allowing the abuse. In spite of her disapproval, I felt since I was getting paid and couldn't feel the pain anyway, I might as well keep the doors to my shop open. That was until I began to gain feelings in my arm and hand during the fourth grade. Momma was very happy but I was a bit disappointed because I knew I would have to permanently shut down my business.

During the fourth grade, things changed even more. After my classmates couldn't pinch me anymore, I was no longer that little popular circus kid. Some of my resentful classmates began to tease and bully me relentlessly. Soon, I again became known as the "Flicked Boy." The bullies loved imitating and picking on me. They would walk with a limp and wave their hands and arms in an uncontrollable motion. The more I cried, the more they harassed and bullied me.

Even though she was completely innocent, I would take out my frustrations on my classmate, Daisy Randolph. When the boys would tease me about liking her, I would react by hitting her just to prove I didn't, even though I was, in fact, smitten by her. Daisy would never even attempt to fight me back. Ironically, through me, she had become a victim of the same kind of harassment I had endured. Thirty years later, our paths would cross and I would have the opportunity to apologize for my insensitive behavior. She revealed she didn't remember any of those immature incidents from our childhood.

In my eyes, my classmate Bubba Ford was the meanest kid that ever lived. Bubba was a stocky, dark-skinned boy who always had a hateful scowl on his face. While the other boys would just tease me, Bubba would take it further by beating up on me. Whenever I looked into his eyes, all I saw was hatred. One day he caught me behind the school and was about to jump all over me. I was always afraid of him but I was more fed up with the beatings and decided that I had run from this monster for the last time. When he drew back to hit me, I swung as hard as I could with my good arm and punched him squarely in the nose. By the reaction on his face, I think he was as shocked as I was. Like a dog with his tail tucked between his legs, Bubba ran into the schoolhouse, crying. Savoring my moment of victory, I soon returned to the world of reality knowing that once Bubba had a chance to regroup, he would look for payback.

The next day when Bubba came onto the playground, all the kids had already heard about my brief stint of bravery and quickly gathered around to watch him get even by beating me down. Since I was no longer afraid, I began clowning and imitating how Bubba was going to beat me up. I would punch myself in the face and immediately fall to the ground. I started a little chant.

"Bubba's going to beat me up!"

"Bubba's going to beat me up!"

"He's going to hit me in the face, knock me down."

"Bubba's going to beat me up!"

"I'm going to tell the teacher."

"I'm going to tell the teacher."

"Bubba's going to beat me up."

"Don't hit me no more, Bubba!"

"Don't hit me no more, Bubba!"

"Bubba's going to beat me up!"

The onlookers were laughing so hard, Bubba just couldn't find the nerve to harass me anymore. Shaking his head and mumbling that I was crazy, Bubba shoved his hands in his pockets and walked away dumbfounded. Without knowing it, I had just become a comedian. Humor would eventually become my most important weapon. A weapon I would use throughout my formative years as well as life. I found by being able to make people laugh, it saved me an untold number of humiliating butt-whippings.

2
FARM BOY

After my last confrontation with Bubba, I really began to enjoy school. Even a part of the four-mile walk to and from school was fun. However, walking along the county highway was scary at times because we had to always be on guard for hateful rednecks passing by in their pickup trucks. They would often throw bottles and other dangerous objects at us as they drove past. We were lucky that none of us were injured or killed. My cousin George or one of the older kids would always be on guard and warn us of any such impending danger.

The last leg of the two-mile walk was on a dirt road to my house. My cousins and I loved picking and eating the wild plums and blueberries that grew along the side of the road. During watermelon season we often borrowed some of the melons from the farms we passed. We would burst them open by smashing them on the ground before eating the sweet center. We would joke and laugh with each other as watermelon juice ran down our cheeks soiling our clothes. Cousin George said we should say we "borrowed" the watermelons. It sounded better than stealing. And when you used the word "borrow," your intent is to return it someday even if you didn't. He was the oldest so we never questioned what he told us. During the rainy days, George would mischievously entice us younger kids to walk through every mud hole we came across causing us to be punished when we arrived home. Momma would constantly scold me for coming home so dirty. Daddy, on the other hand, knew I was just being a boy.

By the time I reached the fifth grade, I was accepted by most of my classmates. Along with comedy, I had discovered another survival strategy, good grades. I was a straight "A" student. During every report card period, most of the kids wanted to see my grades. Being smart seemed to gain the respect of not only teachers and friends but also that of the bullies. I guess having a brain gave me a certain status. My best friend, Eddie Rodgers, was also an "A" student, and he could draw cartoons. Many of the kids were intrigued by his cowboy and Indian drawings.

Eddie was a tall brown-skinned kid with bright red lips. When he walked, he would never swing his arms. It was as if his arms and hands were glued to the sides of his body. We would laugh and tease him but it never seemed to bother him. Even though Eddie and I lived about four miles from each other, we would spend many nights at each other's homes. Eddie loved spending the night at my house because I lived on a farm and he got a chance to help us round up the cows and pigs for feeding. I loved spending the night at Eddie's because his family had a television set. Nobody in my community at that time had the luxury of owning a television. A couple of years later my cousin Bennie, who lived about a hundred yards down the road, bought a television for his family. On Saturday night, practically everybody in the community would go to cousin Bennie's house to watch television. Gunsmoke, a western starring James Arness as Matt Dillon, and The Red Skelton Comedy Hour were my favorite shows. Because there was only one station, there was never any bickering or fighting over what to watch.

When I was in the sixth grade, I persuaded Momma and Dad to let me attend Choctaw County Training High School in Lisman. Butler Public School was for grades first through eight. Lisman was a small community located twenty-five miles southeast of Meridian, Mississippi. Most students transferred to the high school in Lisman when they graduated from Butler Public School. Choctaw County Training School served grades one through twelve. During segregation, schools with the word "Training" in their names were generally known as "colored only" schools. The words, "High School" were designated "white only" schools.

A year later, Eddie would follow me to Lisman where I had met a new friend, Robert Moss. Robert had light brown skin with reddish hair and grey eyes. When Eddie arrived, the three of us became inseparable. We were like The Three Musketeers: when you saw one, you saw the other two. We would become class leaders and every club we joined. We also made it our goal to hold the top offices. We would decide among ourselves who was going to run for president, vice president and secretary. By being officers in the clubs, we always had an opportunity to attend regional and state conferences. Our favorite state conferences were for Future Farmers of America and the 4H Club, which were held at Tuskegee Institute in Tuskegee Institute, Alabama. I was so impressed with my visits to Tuskegee Institute that it was the only college I applied to during my senior year.

Mr. Smith and Mrs. Butler were advisors for all campus clubs at Choctaw County Training School. One or both would drive students to meetings and conferences. The regional 4H meetings were held at Demopolis County Training School. Demopolis was only fifty miles from Lisman but it seemed like a thousand. Most kids living in those rural communities never had the opportunity to travel more than twenty miles from where they lived. Attending school was the most exciting thing that happened in our lives. School served as our academic as well as our social outing. Most students would grow up, marry, raise their families and remain in or near the community where they were born.

I somehow always knew that someday I would eventually leave the back woods of Choctaw County. My father, who had a fourth grade education, had a basic rule in his house, "You are not grown until you get a college degree." Because of this rule, my older brother Lindsey and sister Elaine entered college right after graduating from high school in the late forties. Daddy and Momma were the only parents in the community who were sending their children to college. For some reason other parents didn't have my parents' vision. Momma and Daddy were a family for the entire community. Daddy had promised us that we would have a better life than he had.

Daddy had dreams. Aside from educating his children, one of his major dreams was to own a farm. Prior to farming, Daddy had worked in the back-breaking logging business of cutting down trees with a crosscut manual saw operated by two men. He also worked in the sawmills, but knew that one day his wood cutting skills would no longer be required, and he would be replaced by younger men as well as by more modern equipment. By owning a farm, he also knew that he could support and raise a family, as well as be his own boss.

And to obtain his dream he managed to save enough money to purchase 45 acres of land from the old plantation owners in 1927 for one dollar per acre. Ironically, he never spoke about getting a mule in the deal. He went on to build a four-room house when he and Momma married in the spring of 1928. As a child I thought Daddy built the house all by himself because in my eyes he was a giant capable of anything. However, as I neared manhood, I realized he was only five-feet, seven inches tall and weighed about a hundred and fifty pounds. He was a handsome brown-skinned man with distinct creases in his forehead, especially when he squinted or frowned. I knew he was handsome because I overheard one of the sisters at church on several occasions say, "Deacon Ray sho' is a handsome man." I assumed she was only viewing him in the biblical sense because she would freely say it to Momma. Daddy was always receiving compliments and hugs, from the sisters in the church, for his singing. He and his brothers had a gospel quartet, "The Ray Brothers," and they sang at churches throughout the county. Following in the footsteps of our fathers my brothers, cousins and I sang in the church and school choirs and formed our own quartets.

On the farm my Daddy grew cotton crops which produced spending money and corn and other crops to feed the livestock and the family. We also grew peanuts, sweet potatoes, white potatoes, tomatoes and sugar cane. Syrup for our hot pancakes and biscuits was made from sugar cane. The cornmeal and grits we used for baking and eating were ground from the corn. Chickens, cattle and hogs provided eggs, meat, milk and butter.

Daddy was the most respected man in the community, because he was the only black man who owned a farm. He was also the head deacon at Mt. Olive Baptist Church. Church members were often heard to say, "Preachers may come and preachers may go, but George Ray is here to stay." By owning his own property Daddy was able to provide food and temporary shelter, at no charge, to relatives and members of the community when they were visited by hard times or evicted from their homes. In return he always had a free labor force when he needed help during crop harvesting time and hog killing season.

After Elaine, Lindsey and Lemarvin went away to college we had two extra rooms for families to live in. Momma would spread quilts and feather pillows on the floor for them to sleep on. On occasions there might be five or six family members sprawled across the floor with only a few inches separating them. The rooms were dimly lit by kerosene lamps that spurred a thin film of smoke that covered the ceiling. Some mornings, as many as twelve people would crowd around the breakfast table. Momma always prepared more than enough food to feed them.

My favorite time of the year was hog killing season because several relatives and members of the community came together in what was a winter festival celebrating the end of the harvest season. Entire families would come and help Daddy and we kids would play all day and roast fresh meat over the open fire. There was a ritual to killing hogs. Four weeks prior to the hogs being slaughtered they were put in a pen with a wooden floor and fed corn and vegetables to clean impurities from their bodies. Forty-eight hours prior to being killed they were given only water, to minimize the amount of feces left in the intestines. The day before, Daddy would prepare the area just outside the hog pen by erecting a half filled fifty gallon water drum over a fire pit. Enough firewood was collected to keep the water hot until the last hog was slaughtered. Once the hogs were slaughtered, their bodies would be submerged in the hot water tenderizing their tough skin, thereby making it easy to remove the hair from their bodies. The dressing tables where the hogs were butchered were erected. The hoist that would be used to lift the hogs was tested. Knives were sharpened. Tubs for washing and cleaning the meat were collected and two-twenty gallon cast iron pots used to fry the fat meat that produced lard and cracklings were mounted on cement blocks.

Daddy would select the date to kill the hogs based upon the weather forecast in the World Almanac. The World Almanac was a farmer's best friend because it somewhat accurately predicted the weather for an entire year. Since we didn't have refrigerators, the hogs were always slaughtered in the winter because the cold weather helped preserve the meat and we didn't have to contend with as many flies and insects.

On the chilly morning of the hog killing festival we arose at dawn. Daddy would start a fire under the fifty gallon drum and a small bonfire for people to stand around to keep themselves warm. Momma would prepare her work station where she and the ladies would clean and wash the chitterlings. By seven o'clock in the morning, relatives and friends would assemble and the festival would begin.

Daddy's favorite breed of hogs were the "Hereford," which has a red body and white face, and "The Large White," which has a long body and fine white hair. "The Large White" is known for yielding some of the finest hams of any breed of hogs.

The most exciting time for us boys was watching the hogs being killed. One by one the hogs would be released from the holding pen and they would rush out the edge of the pen expecting to be fed. The hogs were actually walking into a firing range where one of the men or Daddy would be waiting with a .22 caliber rifle to shoot them from close range in the forehead. As gruesome as it might have seemed, we kids enjoyed counting to see how long it would take the hogs to fall. Sometimes they would fall quickly and try to get back up as we counted them out like a boxer being knocked out in the boxing ring. There was always one hog that would have to be shot twice before falling and we would call that hog "Joe Louis" after the great boxing legend.

Immediately, after the hog fell on the ground, one of

the men would jump into the pen and cut his throat so that the blood would quickly drain from his body. The hog, weighing about three hundred pounds, was then hoisted by his hind legs and lifted up out of the pen and held in that position until most of the blood had drained from the body. It was then lowered into the fifty gallon drum of boiling water. After about five minutes, the hog was removed from the water and two men, one on each side using large butchers knives, would shave the hair from the body. While still hanging on the hoist, Daddy would take a large sharp knife and make a surgical cut from the rectum down to the hog's belly and throat. With another man assisting, they would remove the intestines and put them in a tub. The tub would then be taken to Momma's work station and the women working the chitterling detail would begin clearing the intestines of all excess fat and feces. They were washed several times before being packed in large tin cans. After watching this procedure, I would never acquire the taste for chitterlings even though they were considered a delicacy in the black community.

After the disembowelment, the hogs were cut into halves and lowered onto the dressing table where the men would dissect the head, ribs, shoulders, legs and feet. The feet would be cleaned, boiled and placed in large jars with vinegar to make pickled pig feet. The head would be cut opened and the tongue and brains would be removed. The head and ears would be cooked to make a dish called, hog head cheese," a gelatin substance that tasted like vinegar. The brains were often scrambled with eggs and served for breakfast. The tongue would be fried or smothered along with the pork chops. I did love myself some pickled pig feet, but I couldn't stomach the idea of eating hog tongue and brains. The only thing that wasn't eaten on a hog was his hair and hoofs. However, the hoofs were used to make soap.

Throughout the day the air would be filled with conversation and laughter as the men and women harmoniously worked on an assembly line that would have impressed the president of General Motors. By late afternoon, and after all of the work was done, families gathered with their containers and Momma dealt out a hefty portion of pork to each one. Everyone thanked Momma and Daddy for their meat and for being invited, and told them they would definitely return the next year. As the sun began to set in the western sky, the temperature began to rapidly decline and people began heading for their homes as all of us kids played a game of "tag" to prolong the day. Finally, Momma would intervene by kindly telling us that we had played all day and the old folks were tired and ready to go. We were smart enough to know that if she had to speak to us again it would be through a stinging switch branch off one of the peach trees and some of the other mothers would be helping her out.

Life on the farm was hard work for us kids. Our day usually started at 5 a.m. with the feeding of the livestock and milking of the cows. By 6 a.m., Momma would have cooked a hearty breakfast of grits, eggs, sausage, bacon and biscuits on the old wood stove. The aroma of bacon and hot coffee could be detected forty yards from the house causing us to rush and finish our chores and secure our spot at the dining table. I can distinctly recall having syrup and steaming hot biscuits on some mornings. We didn't get paid for doing chores like some of our friends. My parents would make it clear to us that we were already being paid by having a roof over our heads, clothes on our backs and food in our bellies.

Back when Daddy was working for the lumber company, he would leave for work at five in the morning. As with many other fathers in the community, he never owned an automobile so he had to walk the entire eight miles to the mill. When he returned home in the late afternoon, he would further work on the farm until nightfall. On Saturdays, he would work until noon. In his spare time, he would continue to work even more by spending hours walking around the farm, cutting down small scrubs and checking fences ensuring that the animals couldn't get out. He worked so much, I often thought he would work himself to death. Sometimes he would stand and look down on the valley as though he was a king looking over his empire. He was proud of what he had worked so hard to own. Contrary to what many might have believed, the farm was not to be passed down to his children. Daddy's vision was that his farm was going to serve as the "underground railroad" of sort for his children to escape Choctaw County through education.

In order to broaden our horizons, Daddy would bring magazines home for us to read. Via dreamland, I would visit all of the beautiful places and enjoy the many varieties of food pictured in the magazines. He would say we could have that kind of stuff if we would just go to college. When I was five years old, people would ask me what I wanted to be when I grew up, I wouldn't hesitate to say, "A college man." I may not have known exactly what I wanted to be, but I knew I had to go to college to be whatever it was.

Since I was a sickly child, I didn't have to do a lot of the more strenuous farm chores before I was twelve years old. With the use of only one hand, I was somewhat limited in what I could do. Daddy was usually very protective of me. During cotton harvesting season, the family picked cotton all day and I would cry because I wanted to, but couldn't, join them. Eventually, Momma made me a small sack so I could tag along with the family in the fields. However, usually around noon, Daddy would instruct me to play under the shade tree because of the blistering sun.

Since I couldn't participate with the daily work activities, I would spend the rest of the day playing under a big oak tree along a small stream of water that flowed freely through the center of our property. It seemed as though time would stand still as I played with my homemade trucks in the red Alabama clay. Daddy taught me to make my own trucks using a hammer, nails, saw, pliers and 1x12x12 inch boards. I would make the wheels by cutting down a gum tree that was approximately two inches in diameter from which I would cut four cylinders one quarter inch in diameter. I would build a small fire and heat the nail until it became red hot. Using the pliers to hold the nail, I hammered the nail through the center of each cylinder. Using the hot nail I could make a hole without splitting the wooden cylinder, thus making an almost perfect wheel. I then nailed the four wheels onto the four corners of board and rolled my truck off the assembly line.

There was a shallow well from which I drew water to make mud bricks. The mud bricks were used to build a fort where my imaginary soldiers fought against Indian invasions. Workers from nearby fields would come to our well to get their drinking water. Sometimes they would give me a couple of pennies saying it was the best tasting water in the county. On a good week I would be given as much as fifteen cents. Every penny would be spent on Sugar Daddy candy bars and vanilla ice cream, whenever I got the rare opportunity to go into town.

By the age of fourteen, I had gained even more use of my right hand and arm. For years I wanted to plow the fields and drive the horse-driven wagon, but Daddy was still afraid I would get hurt. He didn't think I could adequately control the horse and balance the plow with the limited use of my right hand. I bugged him until he broke down and taught me to plow. Eventually, I proved to be a great help after my sisters and brothers left home. I loved plowing the cotton and cornfields and frequently came home from school and plowed until the sun went down. Commanding the horse to turn left, right, stop and go, gave me a sense of power. Even the smell of the freshly plowed soil and the buzzing of the annoying horse flies and gnats added to the excitement of plowing. I was proud of myself because I felt I was finally making a contribution. And, Daddy was also proud of his baby boy. By the age of sixteen, I could do practically everything around the farm including harnessing up the horses, hooking them up to the wagon, and hauling corn and cotton from the fields.

3
LIVING WITH ELAINE

After the eleventh grade, I again persuaded Momma and Daddy to let me attend school elsewhere. This meant my moving to Louisiana to live with my sister Elaine to finish my last year of high school. Elaine and her husband Edward lived in New Roads, a small town thirty-five miles up the Mississippi River from Baton Rouge. New Roads sat along the banks of the False River, which was three miles west of the Mississippi River. The Native Americans named it the False River because it was a thirteen mile body of water not connected to any other stream or river.

New Roads had a population of two thousand people and two traffic lights. There was a black-owned Mom and Pop grocery store and a "juke joint" (night club) located approximately one-hundred yards from my sister's house. On Saturday nights I couldn't help but sit in the yard listening to various blues bands that kept the community awake until the early hours of the morning. I could only dream about going into such a place. Elaine and Edward were highly respected educators in New Roads, which meant the juke joint was off limits for their newly- transplanted brother.

The high school in New Roads was named Rosenwald High. The school was three single-story brick buildings with large windows and a tall flagpole guarding the main entrance into the campus. Also, there was a circle of beautiful petunia flowers and manicured hedges stretched along the buildings just beneath the windows. The back of the campus hid the library, gymnasium and a football field. There was even a cafeteria with a chef that made cookies that were served on the menu. For a kid who lived in a dirt road farmhouse two miles from the main highway with a population of five people, New Roads was a massive city.

I was excited about attending my new school and potentially meeting new friends. Like a fungus, the word of who I was quickly spread throughout the school, as well as the community. I was going to become a popular kid, but eventually, for the wrong reason. "I was Mrs. Nelson's brother." Elaine taught English and typing at Rosenwald High and was known as one of the most respected teachers in the school. She was also known to demand excellence from her students. My brother-in-law, Edward, was the principal of a local middle school, a few miles away. He later became principal of Rosenwald High in the fall of 1963.

I must say, being Elaine's brother came with a pretty high price tag. It came at the cost of losing my identity. I was no longer Carl Ray. I was Mrs. Nelson's brother and I was always introduced as, "Mrs. Nelson's brother." People could never remember my name. It was always, "Mrs. Nelson's brother." Even to this day when I return to New Roads, I'm still referred to as "Mrs. Nelson's brother." It wasn't easy living in the shadow of my sister and her husband. At all times everybody expected me to act in a respectful and dignified manner. I had to be that "good boy" because of my sister's standing in the community. Girls who started showing any interest in me, would soon back off and justify it with, "You are Mrs. Nelson's brother." I was becoming increasingly resentful of this usual response. I just wanted to be Carl. I began missing Choctaw County Training School where I was my own person with my own identity.

If I walked behind the school building at Choctaw County Training School and the boys were trying to light up a cigarette, nobody would suddenly jump and hide it because "Mrs. Nelson's brother" was coming.

There were even certain kids that I was discouraged from hanging out with because Elaine thought they might be a bad influence on me. Having lived on the farm all of my life, I had not been exposed to the many groups of people that made up the world. One hundred percent of the students that attended Choctaw Training School lived in rural areas and hadn't obtained the edginess of the big city. Elaine even wanted to pick the girls I dated. If she disapproved of a girl she saw me associating with, she would suggest some other so-called respectable family's daughter with whom I usually didn't have anything in common. Abruptly, my lifestyle had changed completely. Elaine and Edward had strict rules. I had to be home in the early evening. Furthermore, everything had to be kept neat in the house including my bedroom. Only opera and classical music were played in their home. This was really traumatic for a young teenager like me who had listened to R&B all of his life. In addition to prohibiting my R&B music, she despised my favorite singer, "The Godfather of Soul," James Brown. With disdain she would say, "The only thing he does is scream." Of course, she preferred me to listen to symphonies or classical music.

Ultimately, I found living with my sister in New Roads was much like I imagined prison. I had lived on the wide-openness of a farm where I was used to hunting, fishing and visiting my cousins two miles down the road anytime I wanted. Symphony music and piano lessons were just not for me. I had to find some people I could really relate to and with whom I had things in common. My two best friends, Donald "Duck" Haynes and Leon Davis, lived only a few houses down the street. Therefore, I had some places to visit that somewhat reminded me of home. Donald's mom owned a collection of comedy albums that we would listen to while she was at work. Through those albums, I was introduced to famous Black comedians such as Pig Meat Markham, Mom's Mabley, and Redd Foxx. Donald and I got the comedy bug and formed a comedy team imitating Pig Meat Markham and Baby Seales. I was Pig Meat and Donald was Baby Seales. We honed and practiced our craft on any kid that wanted to listen. Before the school year was over we were entering talent shows at many of the local schools.

Because I was always looking for some place to hang out during my free time, I adopted the Carter family that lived on my street. The Carters had three children who also attended Rosenwald High. I often used them as an excuse to get out of the house to study, since one of the girls was in my class. Elaine had become a Catholic and thus I was introduced to a new type of religion. People from my community were born Baptist and they died Baptist. The first thing I couldn't help but notice about this "new" religion was that the priest and the nuns were all white and the church membership was totally black. The white Catholic church was located uptown and there were no black members. That arrangement didn't sit well with me. Another thing that didn't sit well with me was the constant raising up and down on my knees and listening to some strange Latin language; so I found a black Baptist church with three hour services, shouting, and good music. The only things I did like about the Catholic church were the services which lasted about an hour; and the beer served on the church grounds during carnival week.

One of my classmates, Joanne Thomas, and her family were also Baptist. Their home became a third place for me to hang out. They were more like country people where I grew up. Betty, Joanne's older sister, was attending Southern University and lived at home on most nights. She treated me as if I was one of her siblings, often inquiring about my grades to make sure I was on the college track. Being pro-college, it seemed as though she was attempting to recruit every good student in the community to attend Southern. Unlike many of my classmates, grades were never a problem for me. I never made a "C" or less in a subject until my senior year. After discovering girls, making straight A's wasn't all that important anymore. Elaine got a little upset after I made a "C" in chemistry. She counted on me graduating as the valedictorian of my class. I had to make the choice of being the valedictorian or being popular with the girls. The girls won.

As the school year progressed, I began to develop my own reputation. I knew that Ms. Maples, the music teacher, was searching for a male to be the lead singer for the school's spring recital. After a couple of weeks of try-outs, she still hadn't found anyone to fit the bill. Since I came from a singing family and had been a member of the school quartet at Choctaw County Training School, I knew I could be the answer to her prayers. So, one afternoon I walked into her classroom and asked if I could audition. I had purposely delayed approaching her, even though I knew that she was in a stressful situation because the opening date was rapidly approaching. She asked me to sing a few lines to a song so that she could get a feel for my voice. I cleared my throat and began singing, "Summer Time." About thirty seconds into the song, I saw the relief overtake her face as she stopped me. Immediately, she instructed one of her students to go and inform the principal, she had found her male singer.

Ms. Maples proceeded to select two female back-up singers, and we began rehearsing shortly thereafter. Two nights a week she would drive us thirty-five miles to the School of Music located on the campus of Southern University in Baton Rouge for rehearsal. I never quite understood why we had to rehearse on a college campus. Perhaps, it was because there was a professional-type sound room or maybe it was because Ms. Maples was also an alumnus of Southern.

Almost like a mini concert, the sound of our music could easily be heard down the hallways of the entire building. College students overhearing our practices' would rush to the music room to hear these high school kids and discuss how good we were sounding. One of the music professors even started his recruitment early by trying to encourage me to enroll in Southern and join the choir upon my graduation from high school. I enjoyed the attention and praise, but Tuskegee had already won that recruiting battle. Aside from knowing my educational future, I had found my own identity by singing and doing comedy.

For the spring recital, I sang, "Wedding Bells Are Ringing." The song was about a guy watching his former sweetheart marching down the aisle to be married to another man. The couple to be married entered the rear of the auditorium and walked down the center aisle to the base of the stage where the bridesmaids and the minister were waiting to marry them. As the mock wedding was taking place, I was on stage singing. Even though I received a standing ovation for my performance, I felt that the highlight of the evening was when Donald and I performed our comedy routine. Elaine also praised me for my singing but as expected, she really did not appreciate the comedy. Anyway my satisfaction didn't come from her acceptance of my comedy, it came from the response and acknowledgement of the audience.

The spring of my senior year of high school was the most exciting time of my entire school career. We were preparing for graduation and the prom. Elaine often inquired about who I was planning to take to the prom. I knew who her favorite prospects were and even though I liked a couple of them, I rebelled and chose a girl that lived fifteen miles from town and a couple of bars down the social ladder. Ultimately, I knew that my choice would get on Elaine's nerves. She retaliated by not allowing me to use her car on my date. But it really didn't matter much to me because I had already arranged for a classmate to chauffer me and my date.

Prom night for me was played out in halves. Elaine was a prom chaperone until 11pm. Upon leaving the prom, she didn't hesitate to remind me of the time I was supposed to be home. The second half of the prom had just begun, and I kept my date and all of my female friends on the dance floor. They were dancing but I was the show. My friends were also waiting for Mrs. Nelson to leave the building so they could get loose. The other chaperones were not as intimidating as Mrs. Nelson. Eventually, I ended up staying out way past curfew and returned home about 3 a.m. tired and with lipstick smeared on my shirt. Knowing that Elaine would make a big deal out of it, I hid the shirt with the intention of washing it when I was home alone. However, when I returned to look in its hiding place, mysteriously, the shirt was gone. Later, I discovered that Elaine had found and washed the shirt. She never discussed or even mentioned the fact that I came home late. Even though I was curious why she didn't, I've learned over the years that some things are better left alone.

On the Saturday before graduation, Donald and I went fishing on the Mississippi River. It was a warm spring day without a cloud in the sky. As we sat on the river bank with our lines dropped in the water, we watched the barges slowly make their way down the river towards

New Orleans. We talked and reminisced about how much fun we had performing our comedy in the school talent shows. In addition to being my comedy partner, Donald was the drummer for a local R&B band. We had aspiration of becoming professional entertainers but didn't have a sound idea of how to achieve our dreams. Even though I was heading off to college and Donald was joining the Army, we promised we would keep in touch and continue to pursue our show business careers. We had a great time even though we caught only one fish. The day was not really about fishing but about saying our good-byes.

Edward and Elaine had driven back home to Alabama to bring Momma and Daddy to New Roads for my graduation ceremony. This was the highlight of their lives. The distance from Mt. Olive and New Roads was three hundred and twenty miles, the farthest distance they had ever traveled from where they were born and raised. Because of finances, they had not been able to attend either Elaine or Lindsey's college graduation in Montgomery, Alabama which was only two hundred miles from home. But I was the baby, and nothing was going to keep them from seeing me walk across that stage and receive my diploma. I noticed Daddy had that same proud look on his face that he wore many times while surveying his farm. Each time one of us graduated, it was actually him, through us, walking across the stage and proudly picking up that "piece of paper," as he called it. Although I was not the valedictorian as Elanie had hoped, in May of 1962, out of a class of ninety-six I graduated sixth, with a 3.8 grade point average.

4
MY FIRST JOB

The day after the ceremony, Ed and Elaine drove us back home to Mt. Olive. I never thought I would be so happy to get back to that farm. My first visit was to see my horse, Buck, in the stable. After giving her a quick rubdown I climbed aboard for a ride around the farm. I rode down into the valley near the creek where the cows were grazing near three baby calves. Daddy planned to sell the calves in the fall to pay for my college tuition. I had a job waiting for me in Meridian, Mississippi at the Holiday Inn, which was just thirty-five miles away. Aunt Jessie, "Momma's sister," who had worked for the hotel for many years, encouraged the powers-that-be to hire me.

During the summer, which passed quickly, I lived with Aunt Jessie and Uncle Ed in Meridian. I worked seven days a week and would even work back-to-back shifts whenever someone on the morning shift wanted to take a day off. My job with the Holiday Inn was my introduction into the real work world of America. The jobs that I held previously were mowing lawns and working in the fields. This job was different. I was working with the public - the white public. I was going to be a busboy which meant interacting with and cleaning up after white people. Aunt Jessie had already informed me of what was expected of me and how to work around white people. I would get the same spiel from the black supervisor, Mr. Miller.

On my first day, I eagerly arrived to work an hour early. I met with Mr. Miller, who was the head chef and supervisor for both of the Holiday Inns in Meridian. Mr. Miller was a large black man with a huge stomach that protruded over his belt like a potbelly stove. My first thought was that he enjoyed his cooking just as much as the customers. I was assigned to work at Holiday Inn South on Highway 45 along with another busboy name Aaron. The first hour was basically an orientation on how to work around white folks. Mr. Miller was firm with his instructions, "Be on your best manners at all times and don't get upset with the customers no matter what they say to you or how they act. You are going to be called boy, so get used to it. I'm 57 years old and I'm still called 'boy.' If I live another twenty years, maybe I'll graduate up to 'uncle.' This is Mississippi and I don't expect any changes during my lifetime. So, welcome to the white mans' world. Dinner break is at five-thirty sharp. You can order anything on the menu you want, but you only going to get a hamburger or a fish sandwich. If the big boss man catches you eating steak, he'll fire you on the spot. Matter of fact, he'll fire everybody in here. Steak is white folks' meat! Remember that!"

Mr. Miller took us to the kitchen to meet the cooks, Chef Beale, Mrs. Fannie Johnson, Mrs. Leathea Jackson and the dishwasher, Robert Earl. Mr. Miller advised us not to believe everything Robert Earl told us. "You know I'm going to train these boys the right way, Boss Man," Robert Earl responded as he took us to the storage room to complete our orientation. Once we were in the privacy of the storage room, Robert Earl started his training. "Welcome, fellas. I have to induct y'all into our little secret society and teach you how to deal with these crackers. Mr. Pete Martin is the Big Boss Man. His office is located at the North Inn, but he comes down here about three times a week to meet with all of the supervisors. Sometimes he doesn't come through the front door. Instead, he'll park in the back and sneak through the loading dock just to see if he can catch somebody goofing off. I think he gets his jollies by firing people on the spot. We call him 'Sneaky Pete' cause that old white man can make less noise than a rat pissin' on a wad of cotton. Y'all see that line up there? It's attached to the door and a small bell inside the kitchen area. Whenever the door opens, the bell tinkles. Whoever hears the bell first, will start singing an old Negro spiritual, Go Down Moses, Move Over Peter or anything they can think of. Then we all start working and singing our asses off. There gonna be some customers that are going to treat you like shit and call you out of your name for no reason at all. That's just the way some white people are. Those dumb asses don't realize you are going to be handling their food before they get it. Don't get upset. Treat them real nice. 'Yes sir, boss!' 'Coming boss!' Then just make your way back to the kitchen and tell the cook, 'special on table five, special on table six' or whatever table it is. Now, come out here and let me show you what they are really going to get," he added with a smirk as he led us to the garbage area just outside the back door where fly-infested spoiled steak and hamburger patties were resting in the garbage bin. He then smiled and said, "Now, this is for those assholes that treat us like shit!"

Next to the restrooms was a large teapot. As we walked back into the area, Mrs. Jackson was removing her hands from inside the pot and replacing the lid. Robert Earl explained her actions. "When you come out of the restroom, make sho' you wash your hands in that tea. You see, it goes with those specials orders. I hope it poisons some of those crackers."

As with most private businesses providing service in the 60's South, all of the work staff was black, except the waitresses and cashiers. Each busboy was assigned to three waitresses. The busboys had to clean and remake their tables as quickly as possible so they could get the customers seated. The waitresses gave the busboys a percentage of their tips. So, it was the busboy's job to make his waitress look good so she would get more tips. We were constantly checking tables to see if the customers needed more coffee, tea or water.

The evening shift was from two in the afternoon until ten at night. The first assignment of the day was to fold cloth napkins to be used in the dining area. There was a closet where the clean tablecloths and napkins were kept. Bussing a table included removing the dirty dishes, silverware, napkins and tablecloths and resetting it for the next customers. Aaron and I often competed on who could tear down and reset tables the quickest.

During my second week on the job, I finally got the opportunity to serve my first special order. That night the dining area was packed and Aaron and I were moving at the speed of light. A Good O'boy, who was there with his family, asked for a refill of water loud enough to be heard by most of the other customers in the restaurant. "Boy, git me some water over here! Seem like I been waitin' an hour and a half. Y'all Niggers is movin' mighty slow tonight!"

Without making eye contact, I bit my tongue and filled his glass as if he didn't exist. His two boys were grinning and enjoying the training session on how to mistreat black folks. His wife seemed to be embarrassed as she focused her attention on the menu. I didn't hesitate to move quickly to the kitchen and yelled, "Special on table three!" I was just in time because Chef Beale was about to start their order. And to add a little extra flavor to their ice tea, I went into the restroom and with a cloth, wiped it on the inside of the urinal before returning to dip it in the teapot. When the waitress served Bubba's klan, Robert Earl and I peeped through the door to see them enjoy a meal fit for a redneck king. I especially got extra satisfaction when they drank the old fashion Southern sweet tea. "Look at that asshole," Robert Earl laughed. "He is really enjoying that special steak and those little cracker boys is smacking on those fly-burgers like there is no tomorrow. Now, I hope they go home and puke all over each other."

That night I discovered just how stupid some white people can be. They would come into the restaurant and insult the very people who were responsible for preparing their food. It probably never even crossed their minds that these same people would retaliate. That's the downside of power. Those with power think everybody loves them, or believe everybody is so afraid that they won't fight back or do anything to harm them. On the contrary, people have been fighting back since the time of slavery. When the plantation owner's barn caught fire, the slave who was right there helping "Massah" put it out, knew exactly who started it. Even to this day whenever I go out to eat, I always treat the restaurant staff with utmost respect. I would hate to unknowingly end up drinking some of my own "special" tea.

5
THE AFTERNOON

I had an exciting summer living with Uncle Ed and Aunt Jessie in Mississippi. Uncle Ed had a hog farm and fed the hogs with leftover food from many of the local restaurants in town. All of the leftover food from the table and kitchen was put into garbage cans, separate from the trash and garbage. He had an arrangement with the hotels to haul away their garbage at no cost; in return they gave him the waste food for his hogs. When we became old enough to drive, Uncle Ed let us boys collect and dump the garbage. I thrilled picking up the garbage because it gave me an opportunity to drive. Daddy had never owned an automobile so driving was an extra bonus for me.

When it came to driving the garbage runs, I knew the routine well because I had made it with Uncle Ed and his sons on many occasions before they left for college. Now that they were in college, my friend, Jerome and I took over the job of collecting the garbage. Since we knew and became closely acquainted with all of the hotel dishwashers and cooks, they gave us all of the free hamburgers we could eat. The cooks would carefully wrap the hamburgers in foil and place them on top of the trash just inside the garbage can. They would give us a quick signal to indicate the can holding our lunch.

During the course of our day, usually our last stop

would be the city dump to unload the paper and other trash. However, before any dumping took place, we would usually park under our favorite oak tree to eat our burgers while talking and laughing about how we out-smarted whitey. After finishing our lunch, we knew it was time to dump the trash and head back to the farm with the hog food. Prior to feeding the hogs, Uncle Ed would cook all of the leftover food, overnight, in large pots heated by propane gas. At first this was confusing but as I look back, I supposed he didn't want his hogs catching any of those "white folks" germs. Back then we looked at much of this as fun time. Life was sometimes great in spite of the oppression blacks endured. And for a black kid from the farm, it didn't get any better than eating a big juicy hamburger with your best friend. Life was so simple.

Summer had quickly passed and before I knew it, on an early September morning, I was preparing to leave for college. After breakfast and cleaning out my footlocker, Momma and I went over the list of things I had to pack for my trip, while Daddy was out working in the field. I was excited as I daydreamed about the long bus ride I would be taking the next day while heading off into my future. This farm boy was going to college to become an engineer, and probably the first black engineer from Choctaw County. At least I never knew of any other one. All of the people I knew that had gone to college eventually became school teachers.

While cleaning out my footlocker and packing, I found a few fire crackers left over from the Fourth of July and shoved them into my pocket before leaving to visit Granny and my cousins. Because we had to get up early to be at the bus station on time, Momma urged me to return home before dark. Moses, my fourteen year-old cousin, tagged along with me to Granny's, who lived about two miles down the dirt road with my Uncle Howard and his eleven children. We both excitedly ran down the dirt road kicking up dust and setting off the firecrackers. Even the singing birds perched on the fences and the tree leaves fluttering about in the breeze appeared excited for me.

A short while later we noticed a pickup truck speeding up the road towards us. We recognized the truck as belonging to Bill Carlisle, a white man whose mother had inherited the plantation from the previous owners. As the old truck came to an abrupt stop before us, Bill jumped out and asked about the gunshots he thought he had heard in the area. I tried to explain to him that we had only shot some firecrackers, but during the confrontation he became angry when I responded with only "yes" and "no" to his questions. With an impatient look on his face, he then asked me didn't I know I was supposed to say "yes sir" and "no sir" to white people. I smartly said "no." The next thing I knew, I was flat on the ground, dazed from a stinging punch to my face. Weighing only 125 pounds, I quickly realized that I was no match for a two-hundred pound plus, former military brute with a bad temper. I instinctively tried to protect myself by covering my face and head with my hands and arms as he stomped at me with his huge feet. After beating and stomping on me, he quickly straddled my chest painfully pinning my arms to the ground with his knees. My already racing heart nearly thumped out of my chest when my watery eyes saw him reach into his pocket and pull out a large pocket knife evidently with the intention to cut or stab me. As he brought down the large silver blade towards my throat, I felt helpless as I stopped struggling and with contempt stared directly into his eyes. It was as if God was intervening and had frozen his hand just before the knife had a chance to slit my throat. Suddenly, a look of embarrassment overtook his face as he stood up and looked down at me for a brief moment before returning to his truck and driving away. Bill's two young sons, who had watched the entire incident from the bed of the truck, seemed to have been in a state of shock. After picking myself up from the ground and regaining my composure, Moses and I ran back towards home as fast as we could. Although exhausted, we didn't stop running until we got back to Moses' house. After catching my breath, I continued on to my house as the humiliation and anger grew inside me. By the time I rushed through the door, I saw nothing but red as I angrily ran to the closet and pulled out the shotgun. Hearing the commotion, Daddy quickly entered the room to investigate. Frantically, I tried to explain what happened as I looked for the shells. After somewhat calming me down, he took the gun and returned it to the closet while urging me to forget about it because in his words, "What was done, was over." And without showing any further emotions, he simply added, "Now come on, we're going to Aunt Dit's house to watch the news." Momma, who had followed Daddy into the room, was concerned and decided to walk with us. By the time we reached Aunt Dit's, I had almost calmed down, but my body was still sore and aching from the beating.

Watching the CBS Evening news with Douglas Edwards was a part of Daddy's daily routine. When we arrived at Aunt Dit's house, oddly Daddy didn't sit inside the house. Instead, he moved her television to the doorway so that he and I could sit on the porch and watch the news. Many years later I would learn that my father somehow had an idea of what was about to happen. It was known that on many occasions black men in the deep South had grown to accept great bodily injury or even death as a way of protecting their families. Thinking back, he had conveniently removed me from our house and access to the shotgun eliminating the possibility of me trying to kill Bill Carlisle or possibly get myself killed while trying to seek revenge.

It was somewhere around 6:10 p.m. when we heard the sound of a vehicle speeding up the dirt road. Before the dust had a chance to settle, we realized it was Bill Carlisle as he pulled up and quickly exited his truck. Knowing there was going to be trouble, I began looking for a weapon to defend ourselves, but the only thing I could find nearby was a glass Clorox bleach bottle. Firmly clutching its neck, I nervously hid the bottle behind my back as I watched Bill slam the door of his truck and walk casually over to the porch where Daddy was sitting. I was standing beside Daddy and thought I was on guard for anything that might happen but as it turned out, I was wrong – deadly wrong. After spitting out a mouthful of chewing tobacco, he pointed at me and told Daddy I would have to leave because I didn't know how to properly talk to white people. "He's going away to college," were the last words Daddy had a chance to utter. In a split second, Bill reached into his back pocket, pulled out a 45 automatic and struck Daddy across the forehead. Without thinking about it, I automatically reacted by striking Bill across his head with the Clorox bottle which shattered into pieces. Our reflexes caused us to lock onto Bill as we tumbled off the porch. While holding both of his hands above his head, Bill cocked the gun and leveled it towards us, but during the struggle, I was somehow thrown slightly to the right of Daddy as a rapid burst of eight shots rang out. Even though both of us were very close to Bill, all eight rounds found their way to the upper part of Daddy's body. When he fell to the ground, Daddy made a large gasp for air and I knew he was gone. Later the autopsy would reveal that some of the bullets entered Daddy's body as he was falling forward towards the ground. The autopsy also revealed that the horrific blow from the gun barrel had shattered Daddy's skull confirming he would have died from the head wound even if Bill hadn't shot him.

The actual confrontation lasted approximately ten seconds but in my mind it seemed like it lasted an eternity. Everything appeared to move in slow motion. The bright flames and thunder that erupted from the gun barrel after each shot were very distinctive and orange in color. The particles from Daddy's clothes appeared to float up in slow motion and mix with the smoke from the gun barrel. His face would grimace each time a bullet pierced his body. His fall was like that of a leaf floating from a tree to the ground during an autumn breeze.

Immediately after Daddy took his last breath, there was total silence and calmness. It seemed as if I was in a vacuum chamber watching a movie without sound. My eyes locked onto Bill as he wiped his forehead where I had struck him with the bottle and looked slowly at his bloody hand. He then blankly peered at me through his Satan-like eyes as I nervously waited for him to turn the gun on me. We stared at each other for a couple of seconds before he finally lowered the gun, turned and walked back to his truck. It was as if he was saying he didn't want my life or maybe it was God who stepped in and saved me again. But at the time all I could think of was, it wasn't me that needed the saving.

After Bill got into his truck and drove away, the calm was suddenly broken and everything began moving at the speed of light as all hell broke loose. Aunt Dit, Moses, and I were totally out of control, crying and screaming. Aunt Dit was calling out to God as she screamed out Daddy's name over and over. On the other hand, Momma's reaction whether from shock or confusion, became our rock as she remained calm throughout the whole ordeal. Maybe God had again stepped in and kept her composed and focused to protect us from Bill. I often wondered what thoughts might have passed through Bill's mind as he witnessed this strong woman in such a controlled peaceful state just seconds after he murdered her husband in cold blood. I imagine her face probably haunted him the rest of his life.

As Momma summoned us around her like a mother hen gathering up her chicks, the first words she said to me in my frantic state were, "You calm down! Don't you do anything! Your Daddy wants you to go to college!" She instructed me to run to town as fast as I could and get the sheriff. We lived about four miles from town if you went down the dirt road to the highway or about three miles if you took the trail through the woods and the valley. Choosing the shorter route, I headed out on the trail screaming and running as fast as I could. About halfway to town, I was totally exhausted and felt I couldn't go any further. Due to fatigue, I became disoriented and appeared to become the same person in two different bodies. When I stopped running and fell to the ground, I saw myself entering the other body. That body continued on running and leaving me behind on the trail. In my mind I was crying out for that body not to leave me. Maybe I was having an out of body experience which is something I had not heard of at that time.

The area where the trail entered into another dirt road, a white family lived. They were outside when I arrived at their house. The old man said he could hear me screaming from a mile away. Fatigued and sobbing uncontrollably, it was difficult for me to coherently explain what had happened. After figuring out what I was saying, he put me in the back seat of his car with his two children and along with his wife, quickly drove me to the sheriff's office. By the time we made it to town Bill had already gotten there and had informed the sheriff that he had in fact killed Daddy. After his arrest the Sheriff checked Bill into the hospital for the wounds he received from the defensive blow I had inflicted on his head. Surely, he had planned to use it as part of an alibi for his trial.

By the time the old man drove me back to the crime scene, both the sheriff and the coroner were already there doing their investigation. A reporter from the local newspaper was also on hand trying his best to interview us; but family members who were trying to calm me down, kept him away from me. I was vomiting so much it felt like my insides were spilling out. Did this reporter actually think I was coherent enough to answer his questions? Some relatives and friends were standing around the perimeter of the yard and on the porch taking it all in. Because it had gotten dark since the shooting, headlights from the cars were being used to illuminate the hedge bush area where Daddy's body was lying. Long after Daddy had been shot, I was still crying and begging him to get up because I was going to college and I wanted him to see me go. I slipped into a daze and began to play a mental game with myself pretending I was having a nightmare and upon waking, everything would be fine. I remembered looking at the people milling about the yard as if I was watching them from high above while a voice in my head was telling me I was still asleep. I would use this nightmare visualization technique until the funeral.

The sheriff and the coroner completed their investigation around 10 p.m. and Daddy's body was finally placed into an ambulance and taken away. Daddy's brothers and other relatives spent the night at our house. The men sat on the porch all night talking and sharing memories. Some of them had bought their shotguns and rifles with them just in case some of the local Klan members decided to show up and celebrate Bill's tragic deed. During the remainder of the evening, the women remained inside the house consoling Momma and Aunt Dit while my cousin Mary, who was a few years younger than I was, grew into womanhood that night. While other kids were playing or sleeping, she was caring and comforting Momma alongside the older women. I would always admire her for the strength that she appeared to have had at such a young age.

The following afternoon my sisters and brothers arrived home. Lemarvin drove from North Carolina to Georgia to ride home with Lindsey. Elaine and Ed drove from New Roads and Louida flew in from New York. Elaine and Lindsey, who appeared to be undaunted by what had happened, began making funeral arrangements. Elaine, the English teacher, was in charge of writing the obituary and Lindsey was responsible for selecting the mortuary and rounding up men to dig the grave.

On Monday, four days after my father's death, a bail hearing for Bill's release was held at the courthouse. Judge Evans reluctantly denied the bail motion supposedly on the grounds that Bill had killed an outstanding member of the community. However, rumor was, the judge really denied the bail to give the black community a few days to cool off, decreasing the chance of some of the family members taking out their revenge on Bill or his family. My family would realize years later that denying bail was just a part of a sinister plan to free Bill after the trial when the public attention waned.

The days leading up to the funeral were spent shutting down the farm and moving furniture out of the house. My brothers, Lindsey and Lemarvin, took charge of selling the livestock and giving Buck, our favorite horse, to a cousin who we knew would take good care of her. Cotton that Daddy had already picked was taken to the cotton gin. Corn, peanuts, sugar cane and the vegetables that were ready to be harvested were given to relatives. Aunt Dit and Moses, who Momma and Daddy took care of, moved in with relatives. Momma had to move from the house she had lived in since she and Daddy were married in 1928 and move in with her sister in Meridian. As far as my fate, I would be dropped off at Tuskegee almost two weeks after school began.

Due to tragic circumstances my life had taken an abrupt turn. I would never again spend another night in the house where I was born and raised. I would never experience the joy of coming home from college for Christmas or any other holiday. I would never experience having my father standing on the porch with that proud smile I had seen on his face whenever my brothers returned home from college or the army. I would never have the opportunity to go on those "God Father" walks around the farm with my father as my brothers had done to receive his advice and guidance before getting married or making any life-long decisions. My complete introduction into manhood by my father would never happen and my life would never be complete.

6
THE TRIAL

Once I saw Daddy's casket in the church, my nightmare was transformed to reality and I again sobbed uncontrollably. The most difficult part was when the casket was lowered into the ground. I had that same feeling of being in a vacuum that I experienced the night he was killed. I vaguely remembered people pulling and talking to me but I was in a different place than they were. I was slipping into a nightmare that would last for nearly forty years. Even now at the age of sixty-seven, the memories are just as vivid as they were that fateful afternoon. I now realize that there is really no such thing as closure. We just learn to live with our nightmares.

A week after the funeral, Lindsey dropped me off at the home of his sister-in-law, Maude Johnson, who lived in Tuskegee, Alabama. Lindsey was returning to his home and family in Albany, Georgia. My brothers and sisters had their families and lives; but I had nowhere to go, even though I was still in a state of shock and not ready to be on my own. The following morning, Maude dropped me off on campus on her way to work at the VA Hospital. Sadly, I had made my transition into college by being dropped off on a street corner and given directions to the Admissions Office. I was utterly consumed by fear and uncertainty as I was about to walk the longest one hundred yards of my life. In reality, the walk was only about five minutes, but in my mind it seemed more like an hour. I was totally oblivious to people, buildings and trees as I made my way up the campus avenue. I had to walk into the office and register myself, report to the housing department and get a room assignment, meet with my academic advisor to select classes, as well as purchase books from the book store. Looking back at the experience, I can't imagine how I made it through that day. Somehow I knew this was not the ordinary way for anyone to begin their college career.

The housing department assigned me a room in Emory Four, a two-story dark brick building located in the southwest corner of the campus. Emory Four was the greatest distance from the cafeteria and academic buildings. This really didn't concern me much because I had decided that I wasn't going to be there very long. My roommate, Eddie Walker, a football player from Mobile, Alabama, was a nice guy. However, I just wasn't quite ready to meet and interact with new people. I never shared my family tragedy with him, nor did I share it with any of my professors. After registering for classes, I would spend most of the next two weeks in my room alone. Eddie had football practice every afternoon and usually wouldn't return to the dorm before 9 p.m. Therefore, he wasn't aware that I wasn't attending any of my classes. I would pretend to be asleep when he came in at night or I would simply just sit out in front of the dorm until he fell asleep.

After two weeks of inactivity, I finally withdrew from school, packed my bags and was sitting on the front porch of Emory Four without a clue on where I was going. Reviewing my options, I was thinking about heading to New York where my sister Louida lived, even though I hadn't asked her permission. As I continued to ponder my situation, I heard my name being called by someone in the hallway informing me I had a telephone call. Ironically, it was Elaine who was calling to let me know I could come back home to New Roads. An hour later, I was on the Greyhound bus for the all-nighter to Baton Rouge. Years later, Elaine would tell me that strangely she had a strong urge that day to go home between her classes to call me. If she had waited until school was out, I would have probably been on a bus heading to New York. I'm sure God prompted her at that exact moment in time, because "The Big Apple" was not the place for me to be.

Returning to New Roads provided me with a comfort zone where I could just let the days pass by without having to think or stress about school. The trial for Bill was scheduled for mid-October so I had to get mentally prepared for the upcoming circus. The hype back in Choctaw was already building because it would be the first time a white person would be prosecuted for taking the life of a black person in the history of Choctaw County, Alabama.

In reality, Waymon Mason, the Circuit Solicitor, had gotten himself in a pickle by filing murder charges against Bill Carlisle. He was all set to make history in Choctaw County by prosecuting a white person for murdering a black man. Initially, he felt that Daddy's case was a Rosa Park's type situation. Daddy was one of the most respected blacks in the county, as well as being a religious figure. Waymon assumed that the white establishment would support him. However, Waymon failed to realize that the whites in Choctaw County wouldn't care if Daddy was Jesus Christ. In those days you just didn't file charges against a white man for killing a black man; that was just un-American. Ultimately, that hasty decision ended Waymon's political career in Choctaw County.

Feeling the pressure of his error along with an underlying effort to save his job, Waymon invited both Momma and me to his office a few days before the trial to discuss his proposition. He began by making a feeble attempt of politeness by asking us to sit down and offering Momma a glass of water of which she kindly refused. One thing that Momma could do well was read devious white folks from a mile away; and she knew Waymon was really a dirty snake, because of his prior history of dealing with blacks in the community. Unbelievable as it may sound, during this meeting Waymon informed Momma that if she would allow me to assassinate Bill Carlisle, he would give up his position as Circuit Solicitor and become my defense attorney. He wouldn't charge us a dime because he was sure he could get me off on self-defense. Momma listened quietly but rejected his offer as the thought entered my mind that this low-down scumbag just wasted our time, as well as insulted our intelligence, with such a ridiculous plan. I guess he thought we were just some naive colored folks who would save his ass. On the contrary, if I had killed Bill Carlisle, it would be no doubt that Waymon would have tried his best to send me to the electric chair or at least led the lynch mob to hang me from a tree. Many years later I discovered that Waymon had also propositioned my brother Lindsey with the same devious plan. After his failure to get any of us to partake in his dirty scheme, he informed Momma and Lindsey that they would have to pay him to prosecute Bill. Caught up in an emotional roller coaster, they paid Waymon two hundred dollars before realizing that public citizens are not required to pay Circuit Solicitors to prosecute lawbreakers. They are paid by the court system. Waymon, behaving like any other immoral white official, seized the opportunity to prey upon the grief of another poor black family. In spite of this, some twenty years later upon his death, he was recognized and remembered as a history maker, the first Circuit Solicitor in Choctaw County to prosecute a white for killing a black.

The day of the trial was more like a circus, just for the

enjoyment of whites; and sadly, it was much like a funeral for many blacks. Vehicles with out-of-state license plates were not allowed in town because the county officials claimed they wanted to keep out potential troublemakers. In reality, they really wanted to prevent any outside media people from capitalizing off any illegal or social injustices that might arise as a result of the trial. A sheriff deputy even stood on the back of a pickup truck with a bull horn ordering out-of-towners to immediately turn around and leave. My Aunts Lee, and Maude; who had driven all the way from Oakland, California to witness the trial were not about to turn and run. They had to park their car in the woods about a mile from town and walk all the way to the courthouse in the blistering hot sun.

The courthouse, as in many southern towns, was located in the middle of the town square. A bronze statue of a Confederate general mounted on a horse was overseeing the front lawn adjacent to a flag pole with both the American and Confederate flags blowing briskly in the wind. A large oak tree was located in each of the four corners of the square. Benches around the base of the trees provided a comfortable shady area for whites. Even though there were no posted "white only" signs as in the case with the drinking fountains and restrooms, somehow blacks knew to keep moving whenever they visited the courthouse square. Uncle Woody would often joke, "Dem trees is hangin' gallows for colored men."

Local blacks who were accustomed to staying in "their place" filed quietly into the courthouse and made their way up the staircase to the hot stuffy balcony. They carried their church fans for a self-made cool breeze as well as weapons to keep the flies at bay. By most people's account, they were prepared to sit through the two trials that were scheduled for that day. The second trial was for another white man, Joe

Carlisle, who had raped his fifteen year-old black babysitter. I am not sure if he and Bill were related, but they probably were since "Carlisle" wasn't one of the most common names in the deep South.

There were no public restrooms in the courthouse for blacks which invariably posed another dilemma. For relief during the trial Momma had to take my aunts about a block away to Dr. Allen's office who was my doctor since birth. While there, the nurse shared with Momma that they really wanted to support us but they could not be seen in public with us because they would be called "Nigger lovers." There was nothing Momma could say except, "yes ma'am."

The trial was a mockery and a downright insult to all black people. The judge opened the trial by scolding Bill and blaming him for the court having had to try him for murder. "There wouldn't have to be a trial if you hadn't killed that old church Nigger. You killed the best Nigger we had. You could have killed any other Nigger and we wouldn't be going through this mess." Even back in racially charred Choctaw County Alabama, I couldn't believe what the judge was saying. And after hearing it, all I could think was, "What was that all about? What was he saying?" In some kind of sick way was he thinking he was paying respect to Daddy? Yet, he only referred to him as, "the good Nigger," "he church Nigger," or "our best Nigger." Was the judge really saying to all of the other blacks in the courtroom that if Bill had killed their father, son or brother, the court would not have to pretend to have a trial? My brother Lemarvin angrily stood up and stormed out of the courtroom before the judge had an opportunity to finish his insulting introduction. Realizing that he was very disturbed, Lindsey and Edward followed him out of the courtroom and caught up with him at his car. Lemarvin had retrieved a rifle from his trunk and was heading back to the courthouse, with the intention of taking out the judge, Bill and his defense attorney, Joe Curl. Fortunately, they were able to stop and calm him down before anyone got hurt or killed. We didn't realize until the trial was over that our cousin George also had smuggled his pistol into the courthouse by hiding it under a body cast he was wearing.

After the trial I was convinced that the term, "Good White Folks," was just a myth, especially in Choctaw County. Waymon was not able to get a single white civilian to be a witness for the prosecution. Mr. Stapps, who was married to the old plantation owner's sister and had lost his portion of the estate to Bill's mother, allegedly checked himself into the hospital in Meridian to keep from testifying. He could have provided sworn testimony as to Bill's past negative behavior and hatred towards my father and other blacks in the community. Sometime after the trial, several whites admitted they had spoken with Bill that afternoon and he informed them he was intending to go to the farm to kill Daddy. I guess in some small way they were trying to ease their guilty conscious. Because of their refusal to speak up earlier, in my eyes they were just as responsible for Daddy's death as Bill. Two white women who knew Momma well made a trip to the house as we were moving and told Momma that the Klan had sent Bill congratulation cards and others were laughing and bragging that Bill had bagged him a Nigger. Then probably to cover their own guilt, they talked about how awful those people were but never realizing they were all one and the same. I often wondered that if they were so good and almighty, why they didn't stand up for us during the trial. Why did all of the so-called "good white folks" suddenly have busy schedules on the day of the trial? In reality, they didn't want to be seen in town with all of the poor white trash. Well… so much for good white folks!

Besides me, the only witnesses for the prosecution were the coroner, sheriff, Momma, and Aunt Dit. It seems as though the trial was only staged to prove that Bill was justified for killing Daddy because I had said "yes" and "no" to him that fatal afternoon. Ultimately, my "yes" and "no" response to Bill's questioning had swept through the county like a wild fire giving white folks a reason to get excited. They could come into town and be a part of the post-lynching party and run the "uppity little Nigger boy" out of town.

Traditionally, Bill's defense attorney Joe Curl was well-known for injecting fear into black witnesses during cross-examination causing them to recant information they had given during direct examination. He was very calm, polite, and calculating when he cross-examined Aunt Dit and Momma, referring to Aunt Dit as "auntie" which was common when whites addressed older black women or "uncle" to older black men. Basically, Joe was saving the fireworks for his cross-examination of me. A few minutes before the trial, Waymon coached us on how to answer questions along with maintaining a low tone of voice so the jury wouldn't think that we were being uppity. "Joe Curl will be trying to get next to you, rile you up and above all he will be trying to trip you up," he warned me.

When I approached the stand to be sworn in, the white spectators began to show their fangs. Because of their stupidity, ignorance, and hatred they were hissing, laughing, and pointing at me as if I was from another planet. Bill, who was leaning back in his chair like a king on his throne, stared coldly at me like he did after he had gunned Daddy down. I stared back at him with one thought on my mind, killing that SOB. My anger grew by the second as I stared back into that sea of hatred, not understanding how they could get so much enjoyment out of my pain. Those scoundrels were finding joy in the murder of my father. I hoped that each one of them would die a slow horrible death, as they saw my eyes defiantly staring back at them from the witness stand. This was like a scene from a movie about the old racist South. In fact, it was like a television reality show in which I was one of the unwilling participants.

After being sworn in, Waymon asked me a few questions before turning me over to be cross-examined by the blood thirsty defense attorney, Joe Curl. Joe was a slender, small man about five-feet- eight with a high pitch southern drawl. He had a reputation of staging theatrical performances whenever there were large numbers of whites attending a trial. Joe didn't disappoint his fans as he immediately ripped into me like a pit-bull into a mailman. Eye-balling me as if I was dirt under his feet, he slowly and methodically began questioning me and making statements in a rapid fire manner. "Boy, who taught you to say 'yes' and 'no' to white folks?"

"Did they teach you that down in Louisiana when you stayed with your sister?"

"You're an uppity little Nigger, ain't you?"

"If you knew how to talk to white folks, your Daddy would still be alive."

"Your Honor, we should take this Nigger to the Mississippi state line and throw him out of the state of Alabama and don't let him back in until he learns how to properly talk to white folks. It's his fault that his daddy got killed."

After hearing Joe Curl utter those words, I felt the rage erupt in me to the point where I wanted to reach out and choke the life out of him. But somehow I found the strength to maintain my composure as the predominately white audience enjoyed Joe's tactics of calling me every type of Nigger he could think of. "Uppity Nigger, smart Nigger, little Nigger." Joe used the word "Nigger" as if it was the first word his mother taught him.

In his ploy to prove that I was an uppity Nigger, Joe asked me four questions at once and demanded that I respond with a "yes" or "no" answer. The answers to two of the questions were, "yes" and "no" to the others.

"Boy did you shoot some firecrackers, set fire to the Carlisle property, and hit my client on the head with a Clorox bottle when you and your Daddy attacked him?"

I attempted to explain that I had shot some fire crackers but I didn't set fire to any property. He abruptly interrupted me with his demand and a repeat of his questions.

"Just give me a "yes" or "no" answer, boy!" Did you shoot some fire crackers, set fire to the Carlisle property, and hit my client on the head with a Clorox bottle when you and your daddy attacked him?"

In no way was I going to give a "yes" or "no" answer to his loaded questions. So I defiantly responded to each question separately, "I shot off some firecrackers. I didn't set fire to no property. I hit him with a bottle and we did not attack him."

Joe appeared to be frustrated as he raised his voice and angered me with his following statement.

"Just give me a "yes" or "no" answer, boy! Now, we know you can say "yes" and "no" because you already said "yes" and "no" to a white man!"

Frustrated, I yelled back, "I ain't never read in no book where it said we have to say, 'yes sir' and 'no sir' to white folks!"

Joe had accomplished his mission. He turned to the jury and said, "I told you he was an uppity Nigger. He's talking back to a white man in court."

He glanced up at the judge and added, "No more questions your Honor" as he strutted back to his table soaking up the laughs and chuckles from his approving white fan club. In the vernacular of a comedian referring to his nightclub performance, "Joe had a killer set." However, the show wasn't over because Joe had orchestrated his own Broadway curtain call. As part of a sinister defense ploy designed by Joe, Bill's wife and kids were allowed to sit with him at the defense table. Just prior to his closing argument one of Bill's sons just happened to be rubbing his father's head and supposedly discovered a small piece of glass imbedded in his scalp. On cue, Joe sprung from his seat and presented it as evidence from the bottle I used to hit Bill with almost two months earlier. The trial proceedings suddenly went from humorous to ridiculous.

When we returned to his office, Waymon showed his disappointment with me for losing my composure and allowing Joe to upset me which he believed may cause the jury to let Bill off. My courtroom behavior wasn't about Joe getting me upset. In reality, it was my personal fight with all the sick demented white folks sitting in the courtroom that got so much enjoyment out of a little "colored" man being murdered and his son being humiliated. These same folks probably go to church each Sunday, get down on their knees and thank their god that one less black man is walking the face of the earth.

As far as losing my composure, I really didn't lose it. I just wasn't going to play the part of the little humble colored boy. They had murdered my father and were trying to put the blame on me. They could have taken me outside and strung me up on one of those oak trees on the courthouse lawn and I still would not have submitted to them. I wasn't going to give up my last ounce of dignity. In my heart, I believed they were not going to find Bill guilty so I was having my final grandstand act of defiance. The older black folks in the community were really proud of me. Years later when I returned to Butler, the one thing they would all talk about, was how I defiantly stood up to the mighty Joe Curl in that courtroom even though they were afraid that I was going to be dragged out of the courthouse and lynched. My elderly cousin Johnnie Ray would always say, "Dem white folks ain't never seen a colored boy stand up to a white man like that. I'm proud of you son. I'm proud!"

About an hour after the trial ended, the news quickly spread across the courthouse lawn that the jury had reached a verdict. Everyone hurried back inside to hear the fate of Bill Carlisle. The audience was silent during the wait for the judge and jury to return to the courtroom. The sound of the squeaky ceiling fans seemed to become louder with each fleeting second. The windows were raised so fresh air would circulate the courtroom causing cigarette smoke from the white section on the first floor to be pushed up into the black section in the balcony. Without vents in the ceiling a cloud of smoke enveloped the entire balcony causing coughs, sneezing, and teary eyes for most onlookers.

After what seemed like an eternity, the judge entered the courtroom followed a short time later by the jury of eleven white men and one elderly black man. I felt the pain of the lone black juror as I observed the fear that was written all over his face.

The judge asked the jury if they had reached a verdict. The foreman stood and said the jury had found Bill Carlisle guilty of second-degree manslaughter. From the groans among the whites, it was obvious that they were in complete disapproval of the verdict and felt that a not-guilty verdict should have been reached. On the other hand, blacks showed very little emotions even though they were also disappointed with the verdict which meant Bill would receive a light sentence for committing a capital crime. Even though the black community tried to find some solace in the unjust verdict, they knew the trial was only a façade and Bill would never spend a day in prison for the cold blooded premeditated murder of my father. They understood that this was the United States of America in the sixties, "Home of the free and land of the brave"… that's if you were white.

7

RETURN TO TUSKEGEE

After the trial, I drifted between Meridian and New Roads, unsure of my educational future. Aunt Jessie made an arrangement with the President of Harris Junior College in Meridian for me to sit in on classes even though I wasn't really enrolled in school. She thought it would be good for me to be around other students instead of sitting in the house all day staring at the walls. I also had friends and cousins that attended Harris Junior College and Harris High School which shared the same campus. One of my friends, Alberta Powell, a senior at Harris High School, lived in the neighborhood where I spent my summers with Aunt Jessie. We sometimes rode the city bus to school and spent our lunch breaks together. Alberta became the first of many angels that God would place in my path as I began a difficult and emotional journey through life. Alberta became my girlfriend and from that relationship I received another angel, Lillie Bell Powell. Reluctantly, I attended but I never felt that I belonged at Harris and shortly after Thanksgiving Day, I went back to New Roads.

Moving between Meridian and New Roads every month didn't help ease my pain or cure my depression. However, attending a Christmas party in New Roads lifted my spirits long enough for me to realize that I wanted to experience the joy and happiness that some of my former high schoolmates felt. I didn't know at the time that joy and happiness were emotions I wouldn't feel until more than thirty years later. I had just begun a living nightmare. Even though I felt uncomfortable at the party, I was motivated to return to college by one incident. My classmate Robert Johnson was talking to Jonrette Richard and appeared to be having the time of his life. Jonrette, who had been a majorette in high school, was pretty. The two of them were attending Grambling State College in Grambling, Louisiana, and sight of him talking to her awakened my competitive spirit. I thought that I was smarter and better looking than Robert, and if he could go to college and talk to a pretty girl like Jonrette, then so could I.

The next day as I sat in the front yard under a pecan tree in my zombie-like state, Edward asked me what I was thinking about. I garnered up enough energy to say, "I want to go back to college." He paused for a moment before asking if I was sure and what had brought on the change of heart. I never told him the truth; that I couldn't stand the fact that Robert was doing something I wasn't doing. Instead, I told him that I just felt ready to get on with my education. In retrospect, I believe God had arranged that little party episode to get me back on track. When I returned to New Roads for my forty-year class reunion, I had planned to share with Robert how he had inspired me to return to college during that 1962 Christmas party. I was saddened to learn that Robert had been tragically killed in an automobile accident five years after graduating from Grambling College.

In January of 1963, I eventually returned to Tuskegee Institute for the spring semester. Mentally, I still wasn't ready but knew I had to try to make a comeback. Somehow I managed to put on a good front as if I was handling Daddy's death just fine. In reality, I was still an emotional wreck and had not even begun to deal with my pain and depression. Elaine and Edward were reluctant in agreeing to my returning to Tuskegee, but in mid-January they put me on a Greyhound bus in Baton Rouge for the twelve-hour journey back to Tuskegee.

Upon arriving back at school, I tried my best to act as a normal student and went to the admission office to get readmitted, and to the registrar's office to pay my tuition and fees, and then to housing to get my dormitory room. Because all of the newer dormitories were full, I was assigned a room in the Cassedy's dormitories. The Cassedy's were dingy white wooden buildings with small rooms and bunk beds and at one time housed the Tuskegee Airmen when they were stationed at Moton Field Airbase in the forties. The outdated bathrooms had long latrines located about three feet off the floor, open shower areas and no doors on the toilet stalls. These building were not built or designed with privacy or comfort in mind. They were cold in the winter and hot in the summer. To keep out the cold drafts during the winter months, students were given clear sheets of plastic to cover the windows and large rugs were placed at the base of the door. When you entered any one of these dorms, you regressed forty years in time.

My roommate, Richard Trent, was a humorous junior from Albany, Georgia majoring in interior decoration. Richard was not the best role model for someone who needed their morale uplifted. On the contrary, he tried to convince me I didn't have to attend my classes' everyday because the instructors had already made up their minds on the grades they were going to give to each student. He would sleep late and advise me to do the same. But I was smart enough to know that engineering required a little more focus than interior decoration. Even Trent's care-free attitude about life would eventually play a role in my on-going recovery because his humor was therapeutic to my soul.

Dr. Fuller, a math professor and Mrs. Willie Mae McGregor, the Director of Basic Studies, would anchor my support system when I returned to Tuskegee. Mr. Henry, Admission Director and Mr. Trammell, Head of the Electrical Department would soon join the group. But in spite of all of my new found support, two weeks after returning to school I was again falling apart and ready to withdraw. I was still having nightmares, crying spells, spacing out and my attention span was less than twenty seconds. I wasn't able to focus long enough to read a paragraph. I would sit at my desk for hours oblivious to the passage of time. I finally realized I was in trouble, so four weeks into the semester, I found myself once again withdrawing from school. Mentally, I could not handle college and made my way to the admissions office to get the withdrawal forms. However, quitting was easier said than done. Any student wanting to officially withdraw from the Institute had to get signatures from the heads of four departments; the academic counselor, the Registrar's Office, the Director of Admissions and the Dean of the School where the student is enrolled. In short, exiting students had to convince each of these educational professionals that their reason for withdrawing was justifiable. And, the job of these professionals was to do everything possible to keep the student in school.

Knowing that it could take at least two or more visits before a counselor would agree to sign my request form, I decided to hit the easy target first, the Registrar, Mr. Davis. Mr. Davis, who resembled Scrooge and was possibly related to him, had no love for students, only their money. I don't even think he loved himself. The session only lasted about twenty seconds after having waited an hour to see him. Upon entering his office, he slowly raised his head and asked, "What you want, boy?" I sheepishly, told him I wanted to go home and needed him to sign my withdrawal forms. He held out his hand as I timidly passed him the forms. Not even taking time to read them, he signed the papers and shoved them back to me and coldly said, "Go home. College ain't for everybody."

Acquiring the other three signatures wouldn't be so simple. I headed off to the Admissions Office to see Mr. Henry who said he was busy and asked me to come back the following day. Upon returning the next day, he spoke with me for nearly twenty minutes about all of the benefits of obtaining a college degree, before he received a telephone call. Claiming it was an important call, he said I would have to come back the next morning and he would approve my request. Even though I was beginning to feel that I was getting the run-a-round, I thought it was okay because I still had to get the Dean of Engineering to sign off. I figured I could be at Mr. Henry's office at eight o'clock the next morning and on the Greyhound bus by five o'clock that afternoon. As I weighed my options, I didn't know where I was going and hadn't informed Elaine that I was quitting school again knowing that she wasn't quite in favor of me returning to school anyway. Furthermore, she and Ed had lost some of their hard-earned money when I hastily withdrew during my first semester, so returning to New Roads was out of the question. Momentarily, I thought I could always go home to Momma but I didn't really want to go back to Meridian because finding a job there would be next to impossible. Furthermore, I didn't want to sit in a classroom at Harris Junior College pretending I was enrolled in college. Also, I couldn't go and live with Lemarvin because he was always on the move and his wife didn't know where he was half of the time. I couldn't go to live with Louida in New York because she was married and the mother of two kids. Lindsey lived in Albany, Georgia with his family. Couldn't go there! Well, I figured I would just work everything out after withdrawing.

Mr. Henry wasn't scheduled to come into the office until 1 p.m. the next day, so that morning I went to see Dr. Dybczak, the Dean of Engineering, who was also my academic counselor. Getting his signature was easier than I expected. He was born and raised in Germany and it appeared that he didn't really know what to say. Maybe our different ethnic backgrounds caused us not to connect. I arrived back at Mr. Henry's office at one o'clock sharp. I could tell, by the first words out of his mouth that my mission was going to take more than a few minutes. He suggested that I sleep on my decision one more night. He bought to my attention that I wouldn't get a refund for the three weeks of room and board that had already been paid for in-advance and since I had a place to eat and sleep, there really was no rush for me to leave immediately. With an inquisitive smirk, he asked me what I was going to do when I got home. My answer was a simple, "nothing!" He then leaned forward over his desk and said, "Run that by me again, boy. You are in a hurry to get home to do nothing?" Then with a slight laugh, he called out to his secretary at her desk just outside his office, "Have you ever heard anything like this, Ms. Johnson? Somebody's in a hurry to get somewhere… and when they get there, they ain't going to do nothing. Does that make any sense to you?" Then looking directly into my face he said, "Boy, you can do nothing around here! You have three weeks room and board all paid up. You don't even have to go to class. You can go to breakfast, then go back to the dorm and sleep all day. If you get tired of doin' nothin', you can come over here and help Ms. Johnson do some filing. And, if you get bored doing that, you can go sit in on a class, so if anybody ever ask you if you ever been to college, you can say "yes" and you won't be lying as you bus those tables at Joe Blow's restaurant making thirty-five cent an hour. Now you think about it, and if you haven't changed your mind in three weeks, I will sign those forms and take you to the bus station myself."

I would spend the next three weeks complaining to every one of my mentors telling them why I couldn't make it in college. They all sounded like a broken record by saying, "you can." After my three-week time-out period and being overcome by "you cans", I submitted and resigned myself to the fact that Tuskegee Institute was not going to allow me to get away, so I dropped my bid to get Mr. Henry to sign my forms. Years later, I realized that Mr. Henry was just conning me. Obviously, he really never intended on signing my withdrawal forms.

Over the next year, I think I heard "you can" a million times! I had my own little joke about all of those old folks and how they must have gone to the "University of You Can." I grew exhausted hearing, "you can." I never really believed I could succeed in college; but, I was just so physically run down by those old folks and their encouragement that I was willing to try anything to get them off my back. And, before I figured it all out, I had graduated from Tuskegee, and was working as an engineer. Those old folks had cleverly tricked me! I guess it's hard to fail when you are getting that much attention, encouragement and love.

8
FIGHTING TO MAINTAIN MY SANITY

After a couple of months living with my roommate, Richard Trent, I decided to move into a room by myself. Living alone probably was not the best choice for me; since it allowed me to further isolate myself and hide my deep dark secret. Unconsciously, I had locked myself off from the world, going only to class, the cafeteria and back to my room. I deliberately avoided meeting and talking to people by focusing my attention towards the ground as I traveled across campus. In the classroom I would usually gaze into my text-book while pretending to be reading. It seemed as though my entire time in class was spent reliving the incident of that dreadful afternoon including that infamous fight with Bill Carlisle. I never understood why, but my math classroom which was located on the second floor in Huntington Hall was very frightening to me. I must have spent ninety percent of my time in that room with my attention fixated on the door expecting at any moment, a gun-toting Bill Carlisle to walk into the classroom searching for me. In my mind I was always planning my escape which sadly included the student I would hide behind when the shooting started. Thoroughly surveying the room, I felt my only other option would be to leap out the window and risk injury in the two-story fall.

During her lecture, Mrs. Christian, my math teacher would periodically walk by my desk and snap her fingers near my face awaking me from my fog. Ironically, it wasn't until she gave her first test that she discovered something was troubling me. Only managing to sign my name, I did not attempt to solve a single problem. Later she revealed to me that she had approached Dr. Fuller to discuss this strange kid in her class that she wasn't able to reach and he briefed her on my family tragedy. Feeling that I was more of a project than a student, he went on to make it clear that he was more concerned about me maintaining my sanity than he was about me passing any of my classes.

My lonely dorm room eventually became a prison where I would spend most of my time sitting in a chair staring into space. Occasionally when I would snap out of my zombie-like state, I would find myself sweating and trembling as if I had seen a ghost. Because I had lost my ability to mentally focus or control my nerves, I spent many days crying. Trapped within the confines of my room, I was not able to stand and walk out of the room. Some forty years later, my therapist would explain to me that I was suffering from severe depression, stress and experiencing mini-nervous breakdowns. During that period of my life, I had no rational knowledge of depressions, stress, breakdowns or any other psychological diagnoses. I just knew my life was miserable. Fearing that I was losing my mind I would ask myself questions and give answers just to see if my answers made any sense. I learned this technique from a passage I once read in a book. It basically said, "If you think you are losing your mind, you are okay. People that are insane do not have the ability to determine that they are losing or have lost their mind." I honestly believed this one statement kept me sane because when I was at my lowest point and felt that I was cracking up, I would repeat it over and over.

Because of my guilt and shame, I didn't want anybody to know what had happened to me. This forced me to have the problem of trying to act like a normal person and at the same time hide what was really going on in my life. I'm not sure why I thought I was acting normal when I never allowed anyone to get close enough to even speak to me. The only people I would have any conversations with were Mrs. Willie Mae McGregor, Mr. Roland Henry and Dr. Joseph Fuller. But in reality, they weren't really conversations because they did all of the talking and I only spoke when I was directly asked a question. Furthermore, I got in the habit of using the least number of words as possible when responding.

Mrs. McGregor, who was a beautiful dark-skin woman about five-feet-four, would eventually become my mother away from home. Being very talkative and energetic, she didn't hesitate to share my story with some of my instructors. Also being aware that I had the habit of hiding out for days at a time in the security of my room, she would send students to check on me. Sometimes I would pretend not to be home and wouldn't answer the door. In response, the student would usually start banging on the door and yelling, "I know you are in there! If you don't open up, I'm going to send Mrs. McGregor over here!" When I would finally open the door, the student would ask how I was doing. Depending on my mood, I would usually manage to utter "okay", "fine" or some other one-word response all the while thinking, "Go away and leave me alone. Let me suffer all by myself."

Mrs. McGregor, or Momma Willie as I called her, had the sixth sense of a loving mother. She somehow knew when I was near my breaking point and would just show up at my dorm room unannounced and would even take me home to stay with her family for a few days or during the weekend. She was married to a school teacher and had two young children who would sit quietly in the family room staring at me as I sat silently in front of the television. Even at their tender ages, it was obvious to them that I had some kind of an emotional problem because I spent most of my time locked up in the bedroom crying. But as if being directed by God, Momma Willie would always come into the room at the appropriate moment to console me. Holding my hand, rubbing my head or laying my head in her lap, she would share her words of wisdom which always would assure me that in time everything was going to be alright. I loved her for not giving me that "be-a-man routine" like many of the insensitive folks from back home who would coldly say, "It's time to grow up now! It's time to be a man! Men don't cry!" I was always told I had to become a man but no one ever took the time to teach me how to become one. I got the impression that a man was mentally strong and didn't reveal his true emotions, and real men especially didn't cry. At that time if being a man would have somehow eased my pain, I would have done anything or paid any price to enter this manhood thing. Momma Willie would say, "It's okay to cry." In fact she encouraged it by saying, "Go ahead and get it out. Remember falling and bruising your knee when you were a little boy? You cried because you were hurting and in pain, but you never realized that you had stopped crying long before your knee had begun to heal. And one day before you knew it, your knee had completely healed hardly leaving a scar. You're wounded now, son. Oh… but one day, all of these tears are going to disappear and this wound is also going to heal." Momma Willie had the uncanny ability to make me see a glimmer of light in my darkest hour.

My greatest task each day was getting up and out of my dorm room where there seemed to have been a negative force that took complete control of my existence. Sometimes I would lie in the corner of my room for hours unable to muster enough energy to stand. I had a weakening sensation inside of me that felt as if there was a giant hand painfully clawing at the walls of my stomach and in an effort to find some relief I would ball up in the fetal position on the floor of my room. After forcing myself to visit the campus hospital, the doctor explained that the clawing sensation in my stomach was the early warning signs of an ailment brought on by stress. Basically, I was diagnosed at the tender age of twenty with having a stomach ulcer.

Dr. Fuller, or "Doc" as most students referred to him, had the ultimate task of getting me to communicate. Doc was a short stocky man about five-feet-six with a partially gray beard. A pipe smoker, who wore a vest, a hounds tooth hat and spoke in a mild but forceful tone of voice. Sometimes after talking for several minutes and not getting a response out of me, Doc would lean back in his chair, light up his pipe and remain silent for long periods of time. I often wondered if he ran out of things to say or was he turning the table on me with his silence. I don't think he had very much experience dealing with students that had problems of my magnitude.

In April of 1963, I was in the third month of the semester and I hadn't developed a relationship with a single student. One afternoon while sitting quietly in Doc's office staring into space, he puffed on his pipe and he gave me the biggest surprise of my young life. He calmly blurted out that I needed a girlfriend. In fact, he went on to say a girl could do more for me than all of the counseling he had given me. He further insisted that I find and invite a young lady to the movies that Saturday night and report back to him the following Monday. I informed him that I didn't know any girls and didn't know anyone who could possibly introduce me to a girl. He replied by telling me it was non-negotiable and it was my homework assignment to select a girl...any girl. Furthermore, he expected to see me back in his office on Monday morning with a report. When I walked out of his office, I felt as if I had just been given a death sentence. I had not even been in a five-minute conservation with any of the guys that lived in my dorm and certainly there was no way I could work up the courage to say anything to a girl. I would stay up almost all night Friday trying to think of an excuse for not going to the movie that might be acceptable to Doc.

Saturday morning after breakfast I found an isolated spot on the top step of Tompkins Hall, near the cafeteria, where I could observe students coming in and going out of the building. From this position I could get a good look at the girls and try to pick out one that I thought wouldn't snap off my head upon approaching her. As I carefully searched the crowd, I found that there were a lot of pretty girls but ultimately I always found reasons not to approach them. After about an hour, I had convinced myself that it was probably too early to ask a girl to go out and I would return to my perch sometime after lunch. But after glutting down my food and returning, I ended up with the same results. Honestly, I would have preferred that Doc would have asked me to shoot myself in the foot or walk on a hot bed of coals. At least it would have been less stressful.

About five-thirty that afternoon I was back hovering in my same spot trying to work up enough courage to complete my assigned mission; but since the movie started at eight o'clock, I realized time was running out. I had seen more than fifty potentials but each time I started to approach one, my feet just wouldn't corporate. Around six o'clock and getting somewhat desperate I observed an attractive young lady walking by herself. By the way she was dressed, she appeared to be an upperclassman which I thought might be good because she probably wouldn't dare go out with a freshman. A million reasons were flashing through my head of why a girl wouldn't go to the movie with me… "She is too pretty for me; too tall; too short; she will probably hate me; she is going to say no; she will laugh in my face; I will not be able to start a conversation."

I had run out of time and knew I had to make my move because at the pace she was walking she would be out of range within a few minutes. After running and catching up with her, God must have taken over because before I knew it, I had said hello, introduced myself, asked her name, and if she would go with me to the movies. It had to be God helping me because I was so nervous it just couldn't have been me. I expected and braced myself for a quick, "no" and figured I would be on my merry way. Much to my surprise, she told me her name was Gwendolyn Adams and if things weren't already complicated enough for me, she said, "yes" followed up with a gentle smile. I quickly and nervously blurted out the time I would pick her up and as I was walking away she asked if I knew what dorm she lived in. Before I could answer, she said, "Olivia Davidson Hall. I'll be in the lobby at seven-thirty."

Sprinting about two hundred yards back to my dorm in what seemed like record time, I went into my room, slammed the door and fell across the bed almost feeling like I was having heart failure. My first thoughts were, "I can't go to the movie with that girl. I don't even know her." Then I remembered I would have to face Doc on Monday. My mind began racing and quickly filled with thoughts of possible excuses I could give him. What would this girl think of me if I stood her up? I quickly came to the conclusion that I had no other choice but to uphold my commitment and take her to the movie which was to be shown in the gymnasium.

Upon picking up Gwen, I had made the mistake of wearing my green Sears' suit and tie only to discover that all of the other movie-goers were dressed casually. This left me feeling like the biggest oddball that had ever lived. Furthermore, sitting in the gymnasium for the two-hour movie seemed like an eternity and the walk to and from the movie was much like a death march. I felt as though every student was staring and laughing at me. I became very angry at her for going to the movie with me because I really believed if she had refused, I wouldn't be going through this agony.

After walking Gwen back to her dorm, I avoided her for the next two years. On campus I would even make an instant detour if I saw her heading towards me just to prevent a confrontation. Even though deep inside I knew it was not her fault, oddly it took several years before I forgave her for inadvertently causing me to have one of the most miserable evenings of my life. Unfortunately, Gwen would die almost forty years later without me having the opportunity to share with her why I never spoke to her again. I now realize the significance of that evening and understand it was the first step out of my personal hell even though at the time, I thought it was just the opposite. Actually, Gwen was one of the many angels that God would place along my path throughout life.

The semester was nearly over and I had never once gone into the recreation center located in the college union. Then one evening after dinner, I mustered up enough courage to go into the basement of the cafeteria where the college union was located. As I stood in the hall looking through the large glass window, I couldn't help but notice how happy the students seemed as they played table tennis, billiards, and cards. I managed to position myself where I wouldn't have to look directly at anyone while watching and secretly wishing

I could be in there with those students who appeared to really be enjoying themselves. Unfortunately, joy was an emotion that had been deleted from my memory bank. After feeling that I had suffered enough through this ordeal, I faded back into darkness and discretely made my way back to my room.

I really hated being alone all of the time, but in my mind it was what I deserved after what I felt I had done. My guilt had been placed in cement back in that Butler courtroom. I had accepted the fact that the corrupt judicial system was right when it said my father's death was my fault so I felt I was just serving out my punishment. As the old folks would say, "You made your bed, now you have to sleep in it."

Surprisingly, one afternoon I garnered up enough nerves to walk into the billiards area of the student union but as always, I managed to position myself in such a way that I wouldn't have to talk or interact with anyone. This technique worked very well until I made my way down into the over-crowded card room where there was standing room only. I stood against the wall and watched the students as they played Bid Whist, a popular card game. Students would slam the cards solidly on the table and boast loudly as the two losers would get up and make way for two other players to take their place. One night a student asked me if I wanted to play. Since the only card game Momma allowed us to play when I was growing up was Old Maids, I told him I didn't know how to play. He told me to sit down so he could teach me the game. Maybe he had noticed me standing alone never talking to anyone and felt sorry for me or maybe he was another one of those angels God was secretly using to do his undercover work.

As he sat beside me, my new friend helped me to arrange the cards in my hand while telling me what to bid and what cards to play. I picked the game up rather quickly and within a few days, I was hitting the table and in a new out-going personality was boasting loudly like all of the other players before me. Every day I would go to dinner at 4:30 p.m. and be in the card room at 5 p.m. and remain there until the card room closed at 10 p.m. I had found something to temporarily keep me out of my personal prison for a few hours every night. I even opened up and began playing cards with the guys that lived in my dorm and would play until the early hours of the morning. Even though I had resigned myself to flunking out of school, I decided I might as well enjoy the last three weeks of my college experience.

When the semester ended in May, expectantly I had earned a "D", and four "F's". But good grades didn't really matter to me because I had already accepted the fact that college wasn't for me and I was going back to my old busboy job at the Holiday Inn in Meridian. However, I was shocked when Mr. Trammell explained to me, that due to the fact that I had only completed one semester, I was being put on academic probation and could return to school for the fall semester. I informed him I wouldn't be coming back because I didn't want to waste my time and any more of my sister's money. He abruptly said he didn't ask for my opinion and told me that I was going to return or he would have security come and drag my butt back. I then realized he had been talking with those other old folks that were always trying to keep me in school. And they were beginning to piss me off! I could understand someone who really didn't know me and thinking that I could succeed in college, but they all knew about my bouts with depression and anxiety. I was emotionally challenged and just wanted them to go away and leave me alone.

9

THE KLAN AND
GEORGE WALLACE

As planned, during the first week of June of my summer break I was back at the Meridian Holiday Inn bussing tables and delivering room service orders. Approximately two weeks upon returning home, I would encounter another life threatening crisis. On the night of June 10, 1963, I delivered a room service order to a room where there were eight white men waiting. When I rose up from setting the tray down, I saw that two of them had maneuvered toward the door. Immediately, I knew something was wrong. One of the men coldly looked into my eyes while telling me they all were members of the Ku Klux Klan and they were on their way to Tuscaloosa, Alabama to support Governor George Wallace who was planning to block the entrance of the black students enrolling in the University of Alabama the following day. Next to my confrontation with Bill Carlisle's knife and gun, the ten minutes they kept me in that room would become the second most frightening experience of my life as they grilled me with questions. "Boy, do you really want to go to school with white kids? Ain't you happy going to school with you' Nigger friends? Do you like that Yankee, Kennedy? Don't you think George Wallace is right?"

As I stood nervously trapped in their room, refusing to

answer, the Klansman went on to say how they knew the "coloreds" down south were happy with the way things are, but it was those Nigger-loving Yankees from up north that were causing all the problems. After they casually discussed killing a few Niggers to keep the rest of us in our place, I was sure I was going to be the first one, as my life flashed before me. Suddenly, I was wishing I had gone to summer school like those old folks had told me. I could have spent the summer in Tuskegee Institute and wouldn't have even seen a single white person. I prayed that if God would get me out of this predicament, I would return to Tuskegee as fast as I could. I was so frightened I could hardly move, and even if I could, I didn't dare think about breaking for the door. It is amazing how much information can flow through one's mind in such a short period of time when they think death is a possibility. I suddenly thought of Emmit Till, the fourteen year-old black boy from Chicago who was killed in Money, Mississippi for just whistling at a white woman and Mack Charles Parker, a young black man who was dragged out of his jail cell in Popularville, Mississippi and brutally lynched for allegedly raping a white woman. Why me? What had I done to deserve this fate? Nine months after Daddy was killed, was it my time? Was I supposed to have been killed along with Daddy? Were these men Satan's soldiers returning to finish the job? Fortunately, my life was spared when the apparent leader of the group nodded his head at his buddies blocking the door. As they stepped aside and opened the door, he coldly looked into my eyes while handing me the money for the order and said, "Boy, you a good Nigger. We gonna let you live. Now, go on and git out of here before I change my mind."

I quickly exited the room and dashed past the swimming pool into the back door of the restaurant. When I burst through the door, Mrs. Jackson was the first person who noticed me and immediately recognized that something was wrong. I guess I must have looked like I had seen a ghost as I trembled and tried to get words to flow out of my nervous mouth. When she summoned Mr. Beale and the other kitchen staff, I told them what had happen. Robert Earl, instantly acting like a house detective, began hitting me with questions.

"What did they do to you, son? What did you tell them?"

"Nothing," I replied. "They were messin' with me, trying to get inside my head. I was thinking about telling them to kiss my ass."

Robert Earl, who was always looking for humor in any situation laughed before asking, "So what did they say when you told them to kiss your ass?"

"I said... I was just thinking about telling them to kiss my ass."

With a slight smirk, Robert Earl then dropped in his punch line. "Oh yeah, if you had told them that, you wouldn't be sitting here on your little narrow ass talking to us now."

"Narrow? What do you mean, narrow?" I asked.

"Boy your ass is so narrow, if I put a dime in each one of your back pockets, they'll jingle together."

Everybody in the kitchen including me broke into uncontrollable laughter. In the flash of an eye, Robert Earl had taken the sting or seriousness out of what I had just experienced and had everybody laughing. In many crisis situations, laughter has often proven to be the only medicine available to soothe the pain that pierced my soul and kept me sane.

No one was really surprised about what happened to me. Such incidents of blacks being harassed and terrorized by whites in the south had drastically increased since George

Wallace had openly declared that the only way blacks would ever enter the University of Alabama was over his dead body. For my safety, Chef Beale suggested that I remain in the kitchen area until it was time to get off. He also advised all of us to be extra careful on our way driving home because the police were always looking for any reason to stop and harass black folks.

Ironically, the only news on television that night focused on George Wallace preparing himself to stand up to the Federal Government and the National Guard the following day. The news coverage appeared to focus only low-class whites as they chanted into the news cameras. They vowed not to let their kids go to school with Niggers and chanted all Niggers should be sent back to Africa. Observing the media circus was troubling me until Uncle Ed calmed me down and explained that Wallace was only putting on an act for his white supporters because he knew he couldn't really stop the federal government from integrating the University.

On the morning of June 11, 1963, the major news story was Governor George Wallace's showdown with the Feds and the National Guard. The customers in the restaurant openly discussed their support of George Wallace and why the government should stay out of state affairs. "The government can't force us to go to school and live with Niggers and we know best how to handle our Niggers," one customer said and he spoke loud enough so that we all could hear his every word.

Aaron and I moved throughout the restaurant as if we were unaware that such hateful people even existed. I was just hoping that they wouldn't venture to ask me my opinion about integrating the University of Alabama because I figured I had already answered enough questions the night before.

On June 12, 1963, the black community was awakened to more tragic news. Medgar Evers, the state's top civil rights leader, had been cowardly assassinated in Jackson, Mississippi. My fears increased as I was still reeling from my close encounter with the Klan two nights before. I was literally sick with fear and just beginning the longest summer of my life as I realized that I had to spend three more months in Mississippi before returning to Tuskegee. I would develop an intense hatred for George Wallace and blame him for what had happened to me, Medgar Evers and many other black people who were beaten or killed during the Civil Rights Movement. George, with his hate-filled speeches, would insight whites to attack blacks during voter registration marches and the federal government did nothing to stop him. This was the same federal government that allowed the arrest of Dr. Martin Luther King and other black leaders just for organizing peaceful voter registration marches.

In what seemed like an eternity, Labor Day weekend finally arrived which meant I was on a Greyhound bus heading back to Tuskegee the following week. As strange as it may have seemed, I had a sense of relief when the bus crossed the state line into Alabama. In spite of the racism and injustice, I never thought I would be so glad to be back in Alabama. When I arrived back on campus, it looked very different as I noticed all of the trees and buildings that had never meant anything to me before. The trees appeared greener and the buildings seemed larger. I guess I had never really appreciated them before since I was always daydreaming about leaving school.

I began the semester by standing in the registration lines with the other returning students. The lines were long but the atmosphere was exciting as I was now able to freely converse with students and exchange information on which teachers to avoid when selecting my classes. Although my mental state had dramatically improved, there would still be many restless nights ahead.

On Sunday, September 15, 1963, I was sent reeling back into reality when the 16th Street Baptist Church in Birmingham, Alabama was bombed killing four little innocent black girls. Like most black Alabamians, I was devastated but I couldn't talk about it because I didn't want anyone to know what had happened to Daddy. My frustration grew as I thought about that S.O.B., George Wallace, believing in my soul that he was the one who actually murdered those girls. I would become obsessed with finding a way to wipe George from the face of the earth. In my mind I would spend days creating different scenarios on how to torture him until he begged for death.

Fear and grief would strike again on November 22, 1963 when President John F. Kennedy was assassinated. I was in my dorm room playing Gin Rummy with a friend when the music on the radio station was interrupted with a news bulletin of that tragic event. Without speaking a word we immediately put the cards down, got up, walked out of the dorm and headed for the college union. Like a fungus the word had quickly spread across campus and teachers began dismissing students from their classes. Girls, traveling across campus, were crying as if they had lost a close family member and there was a silence that covered the campus as many students appeared to be in a state of shock. On this occasion, I wasn't the only one experiencing the pain of hearing tragic news of somebody's loved one getting beaten or killed. In an odd kind of way, I was part of the normal society for a brief moment. I reflected back to my night in the hotel room with the Klan as I imagined how they along with George Wallace and other white racists all across America must have been celebrating the death of President Kennedy.

During the following days most professors didn't hesitate to discuss the assassination of the President and the potential implications it might have upon the Civil Rights Movement. Most of the students and professors on campus were under the opinion that the assassination was somehow linked to the president's liberal views on integration. Looking back, I understand why openly dealing with the assassination in the classroom was more important than any math or science assignment. We were fortunate enough to be taught by black teachers and professors who took the time to deal with social issues that affected our survival in America. They understood that President Kennedy was virtually a rising hero to many blacks and even the students needed to deal with the subconscious stress they were experiencing as a result of his death. Observing how the black community was grieving because of the President's death made me realize the impact he had upon the black community. In my personal opinion, during this period in time, President Kennedy was probably the only white man who was truly loved by most black people.

In his sick mind George Wallace, who might have experienced some satisfaction or enjoyment in the death of the President, also had an unfortunate date with an assassin's bullet. On May 12, 1972 in Laurel, Maryland while campaigning for the Presidency of the United States, Wallace was shot five times by would-be assassin, Arthur Bremer. As a result of the shooting, he was paralyzed from the waist down and confined to a wheel chair until his death on September 14, 1998.

Upon hearing the news of Wallace being shot my first thought was, "The S.O.B. got what he deserved." The fact that he didn't die and was paralyzed gave me even more joy because he would at least have to pay for some of his sins before he died. However, years later when Wallace began to make public apologies and ask the black community for forgiveness for his racist past and behavior, my feeling towards him changed. As strange as it may seem I became a fan of George Wallace as did thousands of other blacks in Alabama. It is difficult to harbor ill feelings towards someone who has the courage to apologize and ask for forgiveness. I often wonder how I and millions of other blacks would feel about America if the President, Congress, Supreme Court and all of the politicians in Washington apologized for slavery, lynching and the Jim Crow era.

10

MENTORS

Even though I resented them at the time, I realized I was blessed to have a core group of old folks who kept me focused and helped me mentally deal with all of the incidents of terrorism t being inflicted upon black people during the Civil Rights Movement. As a way of controlling my anger and outrage, Momma Willie suggested that I refrain from listening to the news or reading newspapers.

Mr. Trammell, head of the electrical department, would become another one of my mentors. He took over as a grandfather figure for most of the students. We loved taking his classes because of his humorous approach to life. He was constantly playing jokes on students. I can vividly recall one incident where he electrically charged an electrolytic capacitor and passed it to an unsuspecting student to examine as he continued lecturing. The charged capacitor which produced a mild electrical shock jolted the student causing him to scream out as he tossed the capacitor aside. I can imagine after doing this time in and time out over the years, Mr. Trammell reveled in leaning his head back and having himself many hearty laughs.

My first encounter with Mr. Trammell occurred one morning as I walked into the Electrical Trades Building on my way to an electrical wiring class. His office was located in a position where he could see students arriving and leaving the building. Upon entering the building, I was distracted by a loud voice calling out to me, "Hey boy! Come in here!"

I slowly approached and entered his office not knowing who he was or why he was summoning me.

"Boy, do you know who I am?" He asked.

Initially, I was startled by the stern looking man behind the heavy voice and didn't know what to say but I managed to mumble, "No Sir."

"I am the HNIC around here!" He said in an enraged voice. "Do you know what that means?"

I had never heard of HNIC and didn't have a clue to what it meant. As I stood both clueless and speechless, he explained in what seemed to be an even louder voice.

"I am the Head Negro In Charge, and don't you forget it!" After a short pause, he broke out in a big laugh and added, "I got you! Didn't I, son? You can go to the bathroom and clean up now."

It was only then that I realized that he was only joking around with me.

Because of his comical wit, Mr. Trammell would become one of my favorite mentors. By sharing his corny jokes, he was always able to get a smile out of me. I will never forget the day I was in his office confiding in him and also crying my heart out because I had to leave school. I just couldn't take the pressure and stress anymore. Suddenly, he stood, looked out of the window and started talking about the girls who were passing the building.

"Boy, look at all of those pretty girls out there. How would you like it if I went out there and brought one of them in here so she could see a big O' baby crying? You know what? I think that's just what I'm going to do."

As Mr. Trammell walked out of the door, I quickly began wiping the tears from my eyes and stopped sniffing before a girl could come in and see me. A couple of minutes later, the door suddenly popped open and in walked Mr. Trammell.

"Fooled you, didn't I, boy?" He laughed. "Next time I'm really going to bring her in here. You don't want the word to get around campus that you are a big cry baby. You will never get a girlfriend. And your Momma will never get any grand kids from you. You have to have a girlfriend to get grand kids. You know what I'm talking about, don't you boy?"

Before I knew it, I would be walking out of his office attempting to stay in school for one more day. Maybe because of his humor, I became attached to Mr. Trammell and saw him almost every day during my four and a half years at Tuskegee.

During the fall semester in 1963, several more teachers and Institute employees would take a special interest in me. I'm not sure if they all knew my story, but each of them served as a part of a support system that would assist me and many other students in graduating from Tuskegee Institute.

I began the new semester with a roommate even though I knew I wasn't going to stay with him long because I was still having severe nightmares and didn't want anyone to know. So, I eventually moved back to the Cassidy's to fester in the heat and cold and accepted my fate of not deserving anything better as my subconscious self-hatred and self-sabotage again took control of my life. Unconsciously I had developed multiple personas, and playing cards would, at times, allow me to become that outgoing person that my fellow students admired and accepted.

Living alone allowed me to become more of a loner as my room became a place where I would spend many sleepless nights balled up into the fetal position on the floor when depression had knocked me down. The severe nightmares, which seemed as real as life, would cause me to fear sleep and lay awake as much as possible. During my nightmares, I had to witness Daddy getting shot over and over again while being locked in a time zone that appeared to last for hours making it nearly impossible for me to wake up. Other times, in a nervous cold sweat, I would wake up screaming. Embarrassingly, I knew the guys next door and in the room below could clearly hear my screams. I soon solved this issue by sleeping uncomfortably upright in a chair instead of my bed to avoid falling into a deep sleep which prolonged the nightmares. Sitting upright in a chair caused almost constant head movement thereby breaking my sleep mode and waking me up before the nightmares could consume me.

Even though I had found a way to temporarily deal with my nightmares, I still occasionally experienced uncontrollable crying spells. In an effort to explain my blood shot eyes after a night of crying, I would get into the shower and wash my hair every morning so that if and when anyone inquired, I would claim shampoo seeped into my eyes. I eventually had to change my "shampoo excuse" when one of the boys suspiciously asked me why I couldn't wash my hair without getting shampoo in my eyes. I then had to get up and leave the dorm while everyone was still asleep and drift around campus to compose myself giving my eyes time to clear up.

During my routine for avoiding sleep, I would often become bored and usually entertained myself by roaming throughout the dormitories in the early morning hours setting traps to surprise students when they got up in the morning. I would round up and half fill trash cans with water and lean them against dorm room doors. When unsuspecting students would open their doors, they would be greeted with water flowing into their room getting their feet and floors wet. I would also take dirty wet mops from the janitor's closet and strategically place them on the doors so they would fall into the faces of students as soon as they open their doors in the morning. My favorite gag was to take a rope and tie the doorknobs of the rooms across from each other making it difficult for students to open their doors. After a few weeks and having been spotted on several occasions dashing in and out of dorms, eventually everyone figured out I was probably the culprit. I didn't mind having my cover blown because my legend was growing and most guys thought my gags were pretty amusing. I was becoming increasingly creative at hiding the lonely little kid and showing the mischievous student that everybody loved.

During my second year at Tuskegee, Thomas (Tommy or TJ) Johnson from Wilma, Alabama, a rural community, near Mobile would become one of my best friends. We were both majoring in Electrical Engineering and took most of our classes together. Tommy, being very focused and having great study habits, would eventually get me involved in study groups and literally force me to study. Leroy Harris from Eutaw, Alabama and Willie Jones from El Dorado, Arkansas, two other members of the study group, would also become my very close friends who tutored me when I needed help. Focusing was a major task for me and most of my time in the study groups was spent daydreaming.

Before Tommy took me under his wings, I would study alone in the auditorium of the School of Veterinary Medicine which was vacant at night but the doors were never locked. Even though I was physically there, I really wasn't studying. Instead, I was mostly spacing out and spending many hours reliving what had happened to Daddy and fighting with Bill Carlisle. I had a non-stop movie playing in my head where I would devise every possible way to torture him. My favorite scenario was where I held him captive in an underground desert jail cell with chains locked around his neck, arms, and legs and lying on the floor in a position making it impossible for him to escape or even commit suicide. Inflecting pain on him in every possible way imaginable, I would always stop short of killing him because my real pleasure was in watching him suffer. I became so absorbed in this routine that sometimes I would go into the auditorium to study but would find myself spending three or four hours playing my mind games and being unaware of the passage of time. Sometimes I would have sat in one position so long my butt would be aching and the page where I opened the book at the beginning of my study session was the same page I was on when I came back to reality. Fortunately, I was smart enough to understand that I was having some serious mental issues and I had to find a way to focus so I would be able to read and retain information. In an effort to achieve my goal, I developed a crude method for retaining information whereby I would read two or three sentences, stand up and walk around my chair while repeating them to myself before sitting back down and testing my memory on what I had read. I would repeat this same procedure again and again, spending an extra hour or more while only making it through a couple of pages.

My emotional situation would take a turn for the worst when I developed a third personality and began experiencing mental black-outs. My first black-out occurred one morning after leaving my dorm on my way to class. Approximately two hours later, I found myself hiding behind some hedges next to the library and having no memory of how I got there or anything else that occurred during the time that had elapsed. The black-outs would occur without warning and if I missed a class I would make up some other excuse knowing that the instructor wouldn't believe some weird story of me blacking out.

I was pretty successful at keeping my little black-out episodes a secret until I was accused of attacking a Residence Assistant (RA). The Cassedy's dorms didn't have mail boxes; therefore, RA's would deliver the mail to each student's room. One afternoon I was awakened by the RA and the dorm counselor when they entered my room with a wild story of which I had no memory. According to the RA, my door was open and I was lying on my bed sound asleep. After placing the mail on my desk, he continued on down the hall and within a few seconds I ran up behind him hitting him twice on the head and back before returning to my room with no explanation. The counselor was shocked at the fact that I maintained that I didn't know what they were talking about and said if I was going to stick to my lie, he had no other choice but to confine me to the dorm for two weeks. Because I was unable to substantiate my claim, I wasn't allowed to attend any sporting events or movies during that two-week period. Confining me to my room was really no big deal because I spent almost all of my time there anyway. I wanted to tell the counselor about my black-outs but I figured he probably would have thought I was just inventing another lie. Even though my black-out episodes presented me with a new problem, I had too many other things going on in my head to lose any sleep on them.

The Cassidy's ended up being home to several mentally challenged and social misfit students. One of the most popular in this group was Marcus Jackson, a Mechanical Engineering student from Birmingham, Alabama. Marcus, a very cunning and intelligent psycho, loved challenging Mrs. Christian, our algebra instructor. After scoring only seventy-five on the first algebra test, Marcus explained to Mrs. Christian that he could have worked every problem on the test but refused to do so because they were too easy and an insult to his intelligence. In order to prove his claim,

Marcus challenged her to give him any problem in the chapter and he would solve it. Unaware of his plan, Mrs. Christian fell into his trap as every equation she wrote on the board, he solved it as if he was adding simple numbers. Marcus' grandstanding before the class was more important to him than earning an "A" on the test.

Marcus' insanity ploys would make him one of the most feared students on campus along with the rumors of him fighting and stabbing a student when he was in high school. He was also an amateur boxer and apparently from his physique, had spent many hours working out in the gym. Marcus' favorite pastime was prancing around the dorm with his shirt off, flexing his muscles and talking to himself. This semi-theatrical performance was a part of him purposely instilling fear into the guys and also another opportunity to substantiate his insanity.

Marcus' biggest meltdown occurred after he received a "C" on a mechanical drawing test in a class taught by a Chinese professor. Upon returning to the dorm, he began screaming and smashing everything in his room. To calm him down, the frightened RA sent for his two brothers who lived in dorms across the street. When they arrived, Marcus screamed even louder at them about how he hated all Chinamen and because God had allowed him to earn only a "C", he wasn't going to believe in Him again. Furthermore, he was going to get him a god that he could really see and if his god allowed him to earn another "C", he was going to kick his ass.

After Marcus' performance in front of the many students who were crowding the hallway, looking and listening through the window, he had validated his insanity and he would have all the guys eating out of his hands from that moment on. This prompted Marcus to begin bullying and demanding "favors" from the guys in our dorm and warning them of the consequences if they didn't comply. He gave specific instructions to his roommate to awake him within two minutes of a certain time every morning, while other guys had to bring him dinners on the weekends at their own expense. Once, three weeks prior to his birthday, Marcus informed everyone in the dorm that he expected them to give him a party with devil's food cake and a gallon of chocolate ice cream. He even gave the assignment of buying the cake to a two-hundred and fifty pound football player. By selecting the football player, he was showing the other guys that everybody was indeed afraid of him. On the night of his birthday when Marcus walked into the dorm, the guys had everything he requested including birthday cards.

I don't know why, but Marcus had never threatened me in any way. Maybe it was because I was quiet or maybe his inner spirit told him that I too was mentally fragile or unbalanced. However, one night while playing cards in my room; Marcus became upset with me because he felt I was cheating. In his calm "God Father" like demeanor, he said he was going to kick my ass. I quickly picked up a hammer that was lying at the end of my bed and blocked my doorway as I nervously said to him, "I ain't taking no ass-whipping from you because I am going to kill your ass right now!" Marcus continued to remain calm as I'm sure he was thinking to himself that oddly the smallest kid in the dorm was defiantly standing up to him. He continued his psychological game by telling me I was too scared and how my hands were shaking like a leaf, so I should put the hammer down and he would just give me a light ass-wiping and get it over with. At that point, I had only one thing on my mind and that was killing that S.O.B. Evidently, by the tone in my voice and the look on my face, it must have been obvious to Marcus and the guys that I had no fear in my heart as Richard Trent finally stepped in between us and announced that the party was over as he asked everyone to leave.

About an hour after my dorm room confrontation, I answered a knock at my door only to find Marcus standing in the doorway with a big smile on his face. He said, "Hey Kid, I like you. You are the first person on this campus that had the guts to stand up to me. If you team up with me, we could rule this campus." He continued to tell me how he had everybody conned and how all of those weak clowns bowed down to him only because they thought he was crazy and if I became his friend, nobody would dare mess with me. Knowing a good business deal when I heard one, I immediately agreed to the partnership.

Whenever Marcus and I were together, it was like the big dog and the little dog show. I was constantly talking trash to everyone, threatening to jump up in their chests and insulting their immediate ancestors. Meanwhile, Marcus would never say a word as he stood powerfully erect and looked around as if he was the king lion of the jungle. I was also smart enough to realize that Marcus couldn't always be with me, so I developed a good con game whenever rivals caught me alone and threatened me with great bodily harm. One of my spiels would be, "Oh, come on fellows! Y'all know I'm just running off at the mouth when I'm hangin' out with Marcus. Y'all know Marcus is crazy and I'm just playing him along. Look at me. I weigh 125 pounds soaking wet. Do you really think I would jump on somebody twice my size? Y'all know I just be bullshitin' around! I would stand a better chance of wearing a pork chop suit while fighting a tiger in a phone booth then beating up one of you guys." Afterwards, I would hear a slight chuckle and knew I had them under my control. Once again I had bought my comedy to the rescue and they melted like ice cream on a hot summer day. I had everybody eating out of my hand including Marcus and my popularity star was still rising as being the funny little man.

The end of the spring semester in May 1964 would be a major turning point in my life. I was finally off academic probation and all of the old folks were so excited for me. They reacted as if I had found a cure for cancer. They gave me hugs and stroked my ego by telling me how proud they were of me and they knew all along I could do it. Soaking up their praise I decided to spend the summer taking classes and working on campus. There would be no returning to the Holiday Inn and the Klan in Meridian.

My summer employment with the campus Building and Grounds Department was not quite the job for a hundred and twenty-five pound kid with polio in his right hand and arm. Our first assignment was unloading office desks and chairs from trucks in ninety-degree heat and high humidity. Under the circumstances, everybody was surprised that I could even lift and move the heavy desks and equipment. To compensate for my weakness, I had developed a technique of shifting the weight of objects to my left hand and using my weaker right hand to balance them. It's like being partially blind in one eye where the good eye compensated for the weakness of the bad eye.

Most of my summer was spent mopping and waxing dormitory rooms, preparing them for the students entering and returning to school for the fall semester. The work was difficult but enjoyable as I worked with a team consisting of eight fellow students and two campus employees. Mr. Lampkins was the supervisor, and he had an assistant name Chappelle. I loved working with Chappelle because he kept us laughing the entire day with his silly jokes, which I would later share with my friends. When the summer job came to an end, Mr. Lampkins let us in on Chappelle's little secret. Chappelle often avoided work by entertaining us with his jokes while we did most of the work, a technique he had used for years. This really didn't matter to me because the jokes more than made up for Chappelle's lack of initiative.

After the summer of 1964, I found myself becoming a new person as my confidence rose and my communication skills returned. Thanks to Chappelle, I was armed with an arsenal of new jokes and had met and developed new relationships with several students. One incident that touched my soul that summer happened on June 21, 1964. Three civil rights workers, James Chaney, Michael Schwerner, and Andrew Goodman were brutally murdered and buried in shallow graves in Philadelphia, Mississippi by the Klan. Momma and I had moved into the neighborhood in Meridian where James Chaney had lived and although I didn't actually know him, the fact that he lived so close to me was upsetting. I was glad that I had not returned to Meridian for the summer.

When the fall semester began in September, I was beginning to take charge of my life and I received a full scholarship including tuition, room, board, books and supplies from the State of Alabama. The scholarship was set aside for all polio victims born in the state of Alabama and the only requirements for receiving it were the completion of one year in college and proof that the applicant was a polio victim. A state representative arranged an appointment for me to take a physical examination at John Andrew Hospital on campus. I met him at the appointed time with my transcript as proof that I had completed thirty hours of course work. My examination was conducted by Dr. Rogers, a light-skin black man who could probably have passed for white in the north. It was also my first time experiencing the class differences within our race. Upon completing the examination, the doctor returned the forms to the state representative and informed him I didn't need a scholarship.

Furthermore, he claimed I was physically able to work and pay my own way through college as he abruptly walked out of the room. Not understanding why he would make such a harsh determination, I was nearly brought to tears. Looking back, I often wondered why he reacted in such a coldhearted manner especially since the money wasn't coming out of his pocket anyway. The representative, who was white, calmed both my fears and frustrations by telling me not to let what the doctor had said upset me because his only job was to confirm that I did in fact have polio. He then gave me a smile and informed me I would get the scholarship regardless of what the doctor thought.

Thankfully, my money problems had been solved and I was no longer a financial burden to Elaine and Edward. I also earned extra money by working in the college union recreational center. Because I was receiving a full scholarship, I did not qualify for the student work study program. Students who did not qualify for work study had to wait at least three weeks after registration to apply for a campus job. If there were jobs remaining, they would be filled on a first-come first-served basis. Since I had become a favorite of the Student Activities Director and her assistants, they made sure they saved a position for me.

During the football and basketball seasons I also worked in the concession stand selling sodas and peanuts and in my spare time, I mowed lawns for several doctors on staff at the campus hospital in addition to receiving a monthly social security check. Because I always had extra spending money, most of the guys thought that I came from a well-to-do family, but I would quickly remind them how many jobs I had. Money was not the driving force for me working numerous jobs, but by staying busy I was able to keep my demons away for longer periods of time. Although they were never far away, I could always feel them lurking around the perimeter of my mind. Somehow these demons knew that sooner or later I would grow physically and mentally tired and become vulnerable to their attacks. Even when depression would paralyze and render me helpless, I was usually able to fight my way back even if it meant retreating to Momma Willie's house for a few days.

Upon returning to campus from my bouts of depressions I would always explain my absence by using comedy so the guys wouldn't really know what I was going through. Once, I told them I had been out partying with three of the finest women in Tuskegee. When asked why I didn't invite them, I simply replied, "I'm too much man for three women and not quite enough for four, but I'm working on it." By the time I finished distracting them with humor, they had forgotten about me being absent from the dorm. I had become a master at covering up my disappearing acts.

With the assistance of Tommy Johnson, Leroy Harris, Willie Jones, and the study groups, I was holding my own in the classroom. Although I still had problems focusing, just by being around other focused guys I was able to improve my study habits. However, if there was no dialogue and each guy was studying a different subject, I would usually open my book and soon drift off to zombie-land without anyone realizing it. Because students in the study group knew each other's exam grades, I was forced to become competitive which soon reflected positively in my overall grades. I didn't want to be known as the guy in the group that was always making the lowest scores on exams.

Now that my confidence and grades had improved, the next goal on my list was the ladies. Using my quick wit and humor, I had amassed a large number of female friends. I was known as the nice little funny guy who didn't pose a threat to the girls because I didn't hit on them for dates. But in reality, my approach was usually from a comedic angle so that if the young lady rejected me, it wasn't like I was really asking her for a date. Often, my approach would go something like, "Baby, if you talk real nice to me, I might let you go to the movie with me tonight." If she responded with, "Ray, I wouldn't go anywhere with you." Well, no harm because in my mind I really didn't ask her to go to the movie in the first place. But if she replied with something like, "Alright, but you have to buy the snacks." Bingo! Thanks to comedy, I had a date.

My first regular girlfriend was Mary Williams. Mary and her friends played cards in the college union every day. Since there was always a shortage of chairs in the card room and because I was small, someone would always share a chair with me. Sharing Mary's chair eventually led to a movie date and her becoming my steady girlfriend. I liked her because she allowed me to be myself, especially when I was loud and rowdy. While walking across campus with her, I would always stop and socialize with everybody while she waited patiently until I finished. But occasionally, she would kindly remind me that it was time to shut up and come on.

My gambling career began with the guys in my dorm when I learned to play a card game called, "Tonk." I would not only become good at playing Tonk, I also became very good at stacking the deck thereby increasing my chances of getting a winning hand. I guess you could say cheating, but back then I didn't consider it cheating; I just enjoyed outsmarting the guys. Rumors began to circulate that I was flunking guys out of school because they gambled with me all night. Isaac C. Cousin from Columbus, Mississippi, was one of my alleged victims but in reality he was his own victim because he never studied. I would arrive in the dorm around one o'clock in the morning after my study group ended only to find Cousin waiting outside of my room ready to engage me in a game of Tonk. We would play until the early hours of the morning. Sometimes he would literally fall asleep during the game which would prompt me to sneak cards out of the deck and spread them on the table and ask if he could beat my hand. After losing all of his money, he would return to his room for bed while I would head off to class for my education. Cousin wasn't aware of the fact that my body required very little sleep.

My room would become a favorite spot for late night gamblers where I provided the entertainment and constant chatter to keep the guys laughing. Using my footlocker for the card table, I would always sit with my back to the window facing the door so that I could see everybody in the room. My humor was more than just for entertainment. By distracting the players with my jokes, I was usually able to take one or two cards from the deck when I was dealing without being detected. The cards would fit firmly beneath the rubber band that circled around the footlocker. In the game of Tonk, the points in the player's hand are added up by the numbers on the cards with ace counting as one point and face cards equaling ten points. When it's one player's turn to play, he has the option of playing or placing his cards on the table to see if anyone has fewer points in their hand then he has. If not, he wins.

I pulled this scam for months, until TJ eventually spotted a couple of face cards in my hand before I placed my cards on the table with two aces that I had swiped from the deck. When he attempted to bring it to the attention of the other players, I quickly stepped on his foot signaling him to remain silent. After the game was over and everybody had left, he remained in my room and demanded that I give him his money back. Since I was a smart businessman, I gladly returned his money plus a few extra dollars and even made him a partner in my little scam.

Overall, the school year 1964-65 was a good one. I

had secured a job on campus between the spring semester and summer school which gave me a place to stay instead of going home, and I would work from June until the fall semester started in September. I stayed on campus from September 1963 until December 1965 without going home. In reality, I didn't have a place to go that felt like home and Tuskegee had really become my new home. There were always a few students who also didn't have homes to go to, so we would spend our holidays together to keep each other from being homesick.

11
BREAKING OUT
OF MY SHELL

In 1963, the Civil Rights Movement was spreading throughout the South and Tuskegee Institute became a staging ground for the civil rights organization known as "SNCC" or Students Nonviolent Coordinating Committee. SNCC voter registration drives and boycotts were usually planned on campus and students would travel with the organization to small towns throughout Alabama to participate in these activities. In early 1965, white students from the north began migrating south to join the movement. Many of these students had to live in vacant dorm rooms on campus.

Having no plans of getting involved because I still had my own issues which I was confronting on a daily bases, I watched from a distance as the movement grew. I occasionally attended an informational meeting just to learn what was happening in the surrounding counties. I never considered taking days off from school and volunteering to march for the cause. When the recruitment part of the meetings began, I would always conveniently exit the building. I had seen enough students returning to campus with head wounds and broken bones from white terrorist groups. In most cases, the injuries were inflicted by the police.

After attending one of the SNCC meetings and hearing Stokley Carmichael speak, I began following the progress of the movement more closely. I decided to get involved after visiting "Tent City" in Lowndes County, Alabama which was located about forty miles west of Montgomery. Blacks who had participated in voter registration marches or registered to vote in the county were retaliated against and evicted from their homes by the white landowners. In response, a black man who owned a ten-acre plot of land allowed these homeless souls to erect tents on his property and live there for free. These displaced people had to live in their tents for almost two years under the most horrible conditions, as well as surviving one of the coldest winters in the history of Alabama. Aside from having no toilet facilities, the grounds were muddy and saturated when it rained and food had to be cooked in large black pots. During the winter, the main source of heat for keeping warm was a large bonfire located in the center of the camp. There were also smaller fires around the perimeter where individual families tried to keep warm. As volunteers, we collected firewood to keep the fires burning twenty-four hours a day. Supporters from as far away as Birmingham, one hundred-twenty miles away, brought in clothes, blankets, food, medicine, water and more firewood.

After returning from Tent City, I informed Momma Willie that I had joined the movement. She suggested that I should limit my involvement because of my emotional state. She felt that I still needed more time to heal and deal with my own emotional problems. Concerned, she also questioned whether I would possibly get injured during the marches. Because of my anger level, she was certain that I wouldn't remain nonviolent and would end up striking back at some of the white terrorists. Momma Willie thought we should pray on it and see what God would tell us to do. I informed her that I wasn't currently communicating with God, because He wasn't around when I needed Him, but she could pray if she wanted.

Before the big march from Selma to Montgomery, Momma Willie's prayers were answered. My passion for marching would change, after I was beaten up in a mock demonstration on campus. The focus of the marches was nonviolence. Therefore, it was crucial that participating marchers did not, under any circumstances, fight back. To insure this, SNCC representatives ran a mini boot camp to train and prepare potential marchers how to protect themselves during an actual demonstration. We were drilled on how to "drop and curl" in a ball to protect ourselves. The young ladies were taught how to protect their breast and the young men on how to protect their groin area while being kicked by the terrorists. Also, we were instructed to always keep moving and never stop to help anyone who fell or was knocked down.

In preparation for the mock demonstration, the leaders of SNCC recruited fifty students to volunteer to play the part of white terrorists and hecklers who would likely line the streets along the route to the state capitol in Montgomery. The would-be hecklers were taken out of the auditorium and given instructions on how to treat us as we marched down the avenue through campus. We were told that this practice would be as close to the real march conditions as possible and we should remain nonviolent at all times.

After the training, approximately two hundred student-marchers filed out of Huntington Hall onto the campus avenue as SNCC representatives with their bullhorns gave explicit instructions to the hecklers and marchers. I really didn't know how realistic this mock demonstration would be, until one of the hecklers approached and punched me squarely in the face. I didn't have a chance to block or duck the blow and my first reaction was to strike back but before I could retaliate, I heard someone on the bullhorn demanding that I not fight back and keep the line moving. Within the next fifty yards, I was repeatedly kicked, knocked down twice, and bleeding from my bottom lip. When I finally managed to break free, I quickly left the line and ran straight to my dorm, ending my short-lived demonstration experience during the Civil Rights Movement.

In the fall of 1965, Alpha Phi Omega, a social service fraternity, was chartered on campus. I had never really considered joining a fraternity until my classmate, Jack Boatman, approached me with the idea. Jack thought that it would be nice to be a part of a service organization because members didn't have to contend with the overzealous hazing that usually took place in regular Greek fraternities. Frankly, I think he also wanted the attention from the girls that came along with being in a fraternity. Jack was convinced that girls were smitten by guys in fraternities. I reluctantly agreed to join with him. We would soon learn that there was very little or no difference between a service fraternity and a Greek fraternity, when it came to hazing.

The charter members, who were mostly made up of guys from regular fraternities, brought their Greek fraternity culture into Alpha Phi Omega. We had to cater to the big brothers as though we were their servants, bringing their meals, washing their cars, shining their shoes, and staying awake all night in the frat house literally getting our butts kicked. I felt the experience was nonsense and I didn't need this to become popular with girls. I had already created my own identity, but choosing not to be a quitter I decided to stay the course.

Eventually, pledging would prove to be an asset for me. I emerged as a confident leader when I earned my "stars" and "stripes" by taking the worst beating ever received by any of the pledges or "little brothers", as we were often called. One night, a fellow pledge and I decided to have a few shots of scotch before heading off to the frat house. Sometime around midnight, Big Brother Hilliard Fraiser stopped by and detected the distinct scent of alcohol on my breath. Since pledges were not allowed to consume alcohol, I was ordered to "point." Point was the position a pledge had to assume while being painfully paddled, which entailed bending over and grabbing your ankle with your butt pointing to the sky.

With the intention of swatting me once for each letter, Brother Hilliard asked me to spell the name of the alcohol I had been drinking. Since that same alcohol had severely impaired my mental ability, I responded by saying, "corn liquor" instead of spelling it. Furthermore, when I bent over, I became so dizzy and disoriented it was no way I was going to be able to spell anything. The constant swats on my butt and my attempts to count each of the painful hits as they were being administered added to my inability to focus. In an attempt to lessen my punishment and pain, my fellow little brothers were trying from the sidelines to persuade me to spell "Gin" or "Rum." But in my inebriated state, I was spewing out any letters that happen to come into my mind. Feeling my agony, my little brothers pleaded with Brother Hilliard to allow them to take some of the hits for me. Another of my little brother was crying and begging Brother Hilliard to stop swatting me. According to my little brothers, I finally manage to spell out, "R. U. M" after almost fifty hits. Like a nearly washed up prize fighter, I had taken a serious beating and I didn't shed a single tear. The severe hazing earned the ultimate respect of my little brothers as well as that of my victors, the big brothers.

My singing ability would also eventually add to my popularity in the fraternity and among the students on campus. During the final week of pledging, aka "HELL Week," all of the pledges from fraternities and sororities would perform on the campus lawns after lunch and dinner. In preparation for the week-long festivities, we were required to spend several hours each night rehearsing songs and dance routines. We were fortunate enough to have some brothers with singing and dancing talent in our group. One of those little brothers was John "Shake" Shaffer, a former member of the famous gospel group, The Five Blind Boys of Alabama. Blending Shake's professional voice with my James Brown imitation created an untouchable duo. Everybody in the fraternity was certain that we would take the first place trophy in the Greek Show singing competition.

In preparation for "HELL Week," we made blue and gold superman capes, blue walking canes, blue and gold paddles, and painted our shoes gold to bottom off our black suits. In an effort to create a James Brown persona, I wore a white cape accented with gold gloves. All fraternities' pledges wore dark shades and shaved heads for the final week of activities.

The performance would start with single-line marching from the frat house, up Campus Avenue to the cafeteria for lunch and dinner while loudly stomping the ground and making the sound of a military cadence. There were thirteen brothers in my line, and as the lead singer I walked at the head of the marching formation. Students lined both sides of the avenue to cheer for the fraternities and sororities as they marched toward the cafeteria. Before leaving the avenue to enter the cafeteria, each group would break out into a performance called the "stomp – marching" routine that included high kicks as the group repeated calls made by the leader of the routine. If we were doing well, the big brothers would always cheer us on.

Upon entering the cafeteria, students would abruptly

stop eating to observe the groups as they circled the building before heading outside to their assigned performing areas. Since everybody was performing at the same time, each group attempted to out-perform the other, in order to entice students to come, watch and cheer for them. The big brothers closely observed the other performances, to see if they were better than we were or if they had more of the students' attention. If it did appear that we were being out performed, we automatically knew it meant longer rehearsals and more hazing.

We closed our performances with my imitation of James Brown singing his popular hit, "Please, Please, Please." Our success was measured by the girls screaming and the guys howling as we left the stage. In concert, when James performed this signature song, he would fall to his knees begging his woman not to leave as he sang in his high pitched voice, "Baby, please don't go." He would then be helped back to his feet by his backup singers who would lead him off stage in a bent over position as he cried, "Please, please, please!" His backup singers would respond to his pleas by singing, "Baby, please don't go!" Near the end of the stage James would suddenly break away from his backup singers, throw his arms in the air and rush back to center stage with his cape falling to the floor while continuing to scream, "Please, please, please!" Before making my final exit, I would pull off my gold gloves and toss them to the screaming girls near the stage.

After all of our hard work and preparation, our dream of performing in the Greek Show was spoiled when one of the fraternities objected to Alpha Pi Omega claiming that we were not a full Greek fraternity but a service fraternity. Two meetings were held with the Greek Council Board to appeal the decision. Unfortunately, we lost both appeals. The truth of the matter was that the word had gotten around that we were a new fraternity on campus and we would probably win the competition because of our strong singing performance.

Our fraternity members, as well as many other students, were angry that we were not allowed to participate in the Greek Show. So, in a show of defiance, we held our own Greek Show performance in the college union the following night and drew a standing room only crowd. In an effort to continue the fight against the Greek Council, we held a parade of cars that drove around the campus, the week after being inducted into the Alpha Phi Omega fraternity. Because, our fraternity brothers had more new and late model cars than any other fraternity on campus, we slowly cruised through campus with every car loaded with pretty girls waving as we honked our horns. We were the new popular boys on the block and we were rubbing it in the faces of the other fraternities.

During my "frat days," I had inherited the fraternity nickname, "Judge Ray." The name came about by chance as we were practicing our songs in preparation for "HELL" week. I didn't have an ending line to one of my songs and in an effort to make the song rhyme I threw in the words, "Because I'm Judge Ray." The nickname stuck as it appeared to give me more respect in the fraternity, especially when the brothers would ask for my opinion on certain topics in frat meetings. I had a special feeling in my heart, whenever I found the brothers sincerely listening and responding to suggestions I offered. Years later, I realized how therapeutic it was for me to join the fraternity. Because of the beating I had endured at the hands of Big Brother Hilliard, along with my humor and singing ability; I became a respected member of the fraternity. You probably will not find "butt paddling" in a therapy guide as a method of dealing with emotional problems, but under the right circumstances there are indeed benefits. The nightmares and bouts of depression were not as frequent, as I began to truly enjoy my college experience.

As I reflect back, the downside of my joining the fraternity was that I would meet and eventually marry Jacqueline Sanders. This turned out to be a marriage literally made in hell. Jackie, who was a member of Gamma Sigma Sigma, the sister sorority to the Alpha Phi Omega fraternity, was employed as a secretary at the VA Hospital. She was not a current student at Tuskegee. Jackie's play brother, Mike Jones, a charter member of the fraternity was part of a scam to get me to date her. I wasn't aware at that time that she was five years older than I was, divorced, and had a four-year old daughter. I already had two girlfriends and wasn't planning on having a relationship with her. The age difference and her having a child weren't important to me.

I developed a reputation in the frat of being the guy that would do almost anything. I had gone into the girls' dorms and sang from the balcony to the students gathered below to watch me. I had even danced in the center of the court, during halftime of basketball games before being escorted off by security to the cheers of the audience. Because I had become a favorite of some of the professors and staff, I was usually allowed to get away with some things that would have gotten the average student disciplined for violating campus rules. Instead of being labeled as a bad kid, I was the little loveable, mischievous kid that caused the "old folks" to just look the other way.

One Saturday afternoon, the frat and sorority had a party at Jackie's apartment and what started out as a joke would end up becoming one of my worst nightmares. My frat brothers were talking about the daredevil things I had done and how I had the nerves to do almost anything. Mike would go on to make a challenge that I should have never accepted because it changed the course of my life. He made a bet with me and the brothers that I wouldn't marry Jackie. Not one to have his bluff called, I decided to go along with the joke and said I would marry her. Mike kept pushing the issue and said that we could go downtown and get a ring and do it right now. Being urged on by the brothers who had consumed a few beers, I stayed the course.

A short time later, three car loads of brothers and sister drove to downtown Tuskegee and bought a ten-dollar ring which as far as I was concerned was the end of the bet. In my opinion, at no point was this charade anything more than a joke and there was no intent on my part to really get married. Furthermore, I thought Jackie was also going along with the joke. I felt so stupid going into the courthouse the following Monday to get a marriage license. I would find out later that Jackie and Mike had planned the whole affair which would cause me to have ill feelings towards Mike for many years, before realizing it was really my own fault. Actually, I had a week and several opportunities to back out of the bet but my reputation was at stake. So the following weekend, we hired a preacher to perform the ceremony. My thoughts during the ceremony was, "Lets' get this over so I can get back to my card game in the college union."

After the ceremony was over, I went back to my dorm and Jackie went back to her apartment. The following day when I saw my girlfriend Mary I said, "Hey baby, guess what I did? I got married!" Mary looked at me and said, "You got married?" I assured her it was a just prank we pulled off at the frat party. I would spend a couple of nights a week with Jackie, but the marriage joke never came up because she knew my two girlfriends. I guess I was literally too ignorant to realize the marriage noose was slowly tightening around my neck.

One afternoon I walked into the lobby of the dorm and

ran into Mr. Harvey, the dorm counselor. He asked me to come into his office because he wanted to talk to me about a rumor he had heard about me getting married. I informed him that one of the brothers called my bluff and I went along with what I thought was a joke. He began questioning me about the steps we took as we played out this joke.

"You got a ring? You got a license? You got a preacher to perform the ceremony?"

After I answered "yes" to all of the above, he said that it pretty much sounded to him like I had gotten married. I assured him that it was all just a joke and I was not married to that woman and, in fact, I didn't really know her. He appeared to be startled by the fact that I really didn't think I was married and when he was able to compose himself, he suggested that I should consider moving in with Jackie. I explained to him I would be graduating at the end of the spring semester and I wasn't getting stuck with a wife. Furthermore, I informed him that going out into the world with a woman was like taking sand to the beach. I thanked him for his concerns and went back to my room, just as naive and happy as I could be. I believed that Mike had told Mr. Harvey about the joke and was responsible for other calls I received from him to persuade me to move in with Jackie.

After several more meetings with Mr. Harvey, I reluctantly agreed to move in with Jackie until I graduated. Once again I assured him that I was leaving town alone. It took me about two months to move out of my dorm room and in with Jackie and the marriage war began almost immediately. The first thing I became aware of was her drinking problem and instant changes in her personality. One night while dressing and getting ready to go out to a local night club, we had a disagreement about some small unimportant issue. Without warning, she reached into her purse and pulled out a gun. Instinctively, I threw a punch and knocked her flat on her back, as the gun sailed across the room. I have often said that I believe God had taken over because I don't know how I was able to react so quickly. I am sure that I had a subconscious flashback to Bill Carlisle pulling a gun out of his pocket, prior to shooting Daddy. Ironically, Jackie appeared to be as shocked by my reaction as I was. I assured her that if she ever pulled a gun on me again I would kill her.

The gun incident was a defining moment in our marriage, and if we had been smart, we would have realized that we both had some dark secrets in our past and should have gone our separate ways that evening. We were about to begin a three year, physical and emotional marriage, with Jackie becoming the only woman I would ever strike. Her mother would also become the only woman I would ever threaten to do great bodily harm.

12
LEAVING TUSKEGEE

In 1965, a federally funded program, Tuskegee Institute Community Educational Program (TICEP), was implemented on campus. TICEP would provide free health care information, summer tutorial classes for students K-12, adult GED classes and lunches for participants. The program covered a nine county area and the work force was made up of mostly students from Tuskegee Institute. Box lunches were prepared daily in the campus cafeteria and transported to the county facilities via trucks and nine passenger station wagons were used to transport tutors. Students who were tutors and drivers received pay for the hours required to drive to and from tutorial sites. Due to the large number of students that went to work for TICEP, the campus work study program was not able to hire enough students to fill campus jobs. Additionally, TICEP paid considerably more than campus work study jobs. I would eventually work for TICEP three days per week and in the college union four nights per week.

While working with TICEP, I became both a tutor and driver and was assigned to Lowndes County, one of the most violent counties in Alabama during the Civil Rights Movement. A matter of fact, Viola Liuzzo and Jonathan Myrick Daniels were two white activists from the North who were killed in Lowndes County during the movement.

On March 25, 1965, Viola a mother of five from Michigan was murdered by members of the Ku Klux Klan as she drove along the highway between Selma and Montgomery. Jonathan, a priest from Keene, New Hampshire, was killed by a volunteer deputy in Hayneville after he and twenty-eight other protestors were released from serving six days in jail. The trigger-happy deputy attempted to shoot a seventeen year-old black female protestor who was trying to buy a soft drink from a local store. Jonathan stepped in front of the girl as the deputy pulled the trigger of the shotgun and was instantly killed. During the trials, the murderers of Viola and Jonathan were acquitted by all white juries.

The tutorial program was held in a church eighty miles from Tuskegee and I was paid four hours a day for driving and three hours for tutoring. There were major safety issues involved in working and commuting to centers in communities up to one hundred miles away from campus. Of course local law officials and hateful whites were aware of these centers and that they were being staffed and operated by "outsiders" as we were often called. We were subjected to daily harassment, which occurred mostly at night during our commute back to Tuskegee. Harassment from the deputies usually came in the form of traffic violations. Even though drivers were instructed to always obey the speed limits, the sheriff deputies didn't hesitate to create their own traffic violations. We often received tickets for failing to dim our headlights, broken tail-lights, driving too slow, reckless driving, and running imaginary stop signs when there were none. On other occasions, the deputies would trail us until we crossed their county line or reached a major highway. The white terrorist or the "good O'boys" had their own tactic of harassment by passing us in their pick-ups, while yelling out obscenities and hurling beer bottles and cans at us as they drove by.

During the TICEP Program, Steve and Amelia, two white students from St. Olaf College in Minnesota, moved down to participate in the movement. They soon transferred to the Tuskegee Institute, became tutors, and were assigned to Lowndes County. Due to the anticipated harassment by the deputies, none of the drivers wanted white students riding with them in their cars. In light of this, every afternoon all of the drivers would try to quickly fill their cars with at least eight students before Steve and Amelia would arrive for the departure to Lowndes County. Those drivers who were "lucky" enough to get one of the white students knew that there was a standard routine for transporting them. The student had to ride in the middle seat and always be ready to duck down on the floor, whenever a Sheriff's car was spotted patrolling the highway. The deputies appeared to get special satisfaction whenever they detained a car with a white student. Many times he or she would be ordered out of the car and interrogated, while being called such things as "Yankee" and "Nigger-lover" and demanded that they go back to the North. The constant harassment by the deputies was just an expected hazard of the job, and most of the unjustified traffic tickets were paid by the TICEP program. Looking back, I considered myself fortunate not to have been killed or hurt, as I would continue to work for TICEP until the beginning of the spring semester of 1967. Because I had begun applying for employment in September of my senior year, I became the first student in my class to receive a job offer. So, in February of the next year I received an offer from Lockheed Missiles and Space Company in Sunnyvale, California. I was very excited and shared the offer letter with my electronics instructor who in turn, shared my good news with the class. However, before the semester ended, four other classmates including TJ, had also accepted offers from Lockheed.

In the midst of my excitement of receiving a viable job offer and making preparation for graduation, I would experience my worst mental black-out and nearly killed Jackie during the ordeal. On the night of the blackout I had gone to bed before Jackie. When I woke up, I found that I had knocked her unconscious and was sitting across her chest with the lamp from the night stand in my hand. Fortunately, I snapped out of my aggressive state before I had an opportunity to smash the lamp onto her head. I don't remember what I was saying, but I was screaming so loudly the neighbors from next door and across the street had gathered in the yard. Some of them were banging on my window trying to get my attention. Still in a state of shock, I managed to open the door as my next door neighbor rushed in and began reviving Jackie.

When Jackie regained consciousness, she was nearly frightened to death but, thankfully, she believed me when I told her I didn't remember attacking her. We tried to piece together the events leading up to the attack, as I didn't remember being angry with her when I went to bed. She explained that she was standing by the bed after taking a couple of aspirins when I, without provocation, jumped out of bed and grabbed her. That was the last thing she could remember. I must have been in my black-out state for several minutes because the room was torn apart and neither one of us remembered me doing it.

Ironically, it would be in the early 90's before I heard of a similar occurrence being shared on a television news show. There was a gentleman being interviewed on 60 Minutes who had reportedly killed his wife but maintained he did not remember the incident. Since he and his wife had been married for many years with no history or evidence of marital problems, there were no obvious motives for him to take her life. I knew exactly what he was experiencing, because he was telling my story and I was feeling his pain.

On May 21, 1967, graduation day had finally arrived. The final week was spent checking with my advisor to ensure that the professors had turned in my final grades. I also received financial clearance from the Provost office stating that I had no pending debts to the Institute. The most exciting time of that week was rehearsing for the graduation ceremony. There was a sense of freedom, as if I had just escaped from prison. The air was filled with joy, as everybody talked of their plans for the future and not having to see their most hated professors again.

In preparation for the graduation I drove to Meridian and brought Momma back to Tuskegee. Lindsey, who earlier had moved from Georgia to Montgomery, came with his family along with Jackie, her daughter Vicki and my mother-in-law, to see me pick up the greatest prize of my life. However, the jubilation of graduation was soon dampened as I observed Momma sitting alone at the breakfast table that Sunday morning. I felt that she was thinking about Daddy missing this momentous occasion and sadness overtook me. I quickly gathered my composure and hid my feelings by pretending to be excited. With watery eyes, I rushed out of the apartment heading to the gas station, even though my fuel tank was already full.

The graduation ceremony was held on the lawn between Tompkins Hall, the cafeteria, and White Hall, which housed the girls' dormitory. At nine o'clock that morning, approximately five-hundred, soon-to-be alums, lined up to make their final walk across the lawn as college students. Family members and friends were scrambling for folding chairs, as seating was on a first-come-first-served basis. The first order of business for each student in the procession was to locate his or her family members in the audience and solicit cheers and waves of approval. As I neared the area where my family sat, Jackie excitedly jumped out of her seat and hurriedly brushed by a group of attendees to take my picture.

After enduring a boring speaker embracing a topic we probably wouldn't remember the next day, the moment that the future graduates were waiting for finally arrived. With a quick switch of our tassels from the left to the right side of our caps, we were declared the 1967 graduates of Tuskegee Institute – a distinction of which I am still proud of today. Afterward, the celebrations began early with the traditional dancing and shouting among the new graduates. Even though the president asked that we compose ourselves until we had marched across the stage to receive our diplomas, there still were a few graduates who just had to use the moment to put on their personal, mini-Broadway performances, while receiving extra attention and applause from the audience. Some had even choreographed special walks, bows, waves or dances that only lasted a few seconds but would set them apart from the crowd and give them their moment of fame. When the benediction was finally given, there were hugs and good-byes among the graduates, as each of us feathered out to locate our families for more praise, congratulations, and of course the customary posing for pictures. We would be heading out into the world to begin our careers and start families. To avoid going to Vietnam, several of my friends made plans to attend graduate school so they would be granted a deferment. Unfortunately for many, there was no way to avoid being dragged into an unpopular war and at least six would die and two that would end up seriously wounded and rendered to wheel chairs for the rest of their lives.

13
CALIFORNIA HERE I COME

After graduation I had a month before reporting to Lockheed in Sunnyvale, California. Jackie, Vicki and I made plans for our transition to our new world as we agreed that they would remain in Tuskegee until I found an apartment. Even though TJ and I decided that we would drive our cars on our journey west, we were not alone. Ellis Jones from Pensacola, Florida and Wilbert Crockett from Jackson, Mississippi, who had also been hired by Lockheed, would share the ride with us. TJ also brought his sixteen-year old brother, James, with him. We all met up on June 19, 1967, and spent the night at Wilbert's home in Jackson. Early the next morning, we would begin our carpool to California…. or the "promise land" as the old black folks would say, even though most of them had never traveled more than fifty-miles from their birthplace.

We would still face challenges before we arrived in our new homeland. We didn't realize that blacks were still not allowed to stay in hotels, even though the Civil Rights Act forbidding such discriminations had become law in 1965. Sometime around midnight of our first night we attempted to check into a Holiday Inn in Amarillo, Texas only to be informed that there were no rooms available even though the neon signs outside clearly stated there were vacancies. Next door, there was a Ramada Inn also with a vacancy sign but we were told that they too did not have any vacancies. Furthermore, the clerk at the registration desk didn't hesitate to inform us that there were no hotel rooms available in Amarillo, due to a convention in town. She was also "kind" enough to inform us that there were rooms probably available in a town that we passed through about fifty-miles before arriving in Amarillo. She seemed, conveniently, not to know the name of the town. It was obvious that she was so frightened at the sight of five weary black guys she was unaware of what was coming out of her mouth. After visiting three other motels also with vacancies signs and being told the same lie, the fellas insisted that we should continue driving because it was obvious that no motel was going to rent to blacks. I was so tired and angry that I assured them that we were going to sleep in a bed in Amarillo, even if the bed was in jail. On the verge of retaliation, I was looking for a rock or brick to hurl through somebody's window when one of the guys spotted a sign in the window of a run-down motel just across the street. It read, "Wake me… I need the Money." Surprisingly, the owner of the motel not only rented us two rooms, he was also kind enough to allow to us stay over until we woke up, which was around two the following afternoon.

The night after leaving Amarillo, we would have another incident that would give us incentive to continue driving non-stop. After night fell and while still in Texas, we were traveling on an unpaved section of the highway when a pickup truck approached us from the rear at a reckless and rapid pace. Because I was driving ahead of TJ, I began to slow down so the truck could pass both of our cars at once. However, instead of passing us, the driver of the truck began to tailgate TJ's car. As I accelerated, the truck driver continued to drive a few feet behind his car. Alarmed, TJ pulled alongside of my car and yelled that the guys were chasing and harassing us and we should try losing them. For several miles, we reached speeds in access of eighty miles per hour on the narrow road. I prayed for a cop to appear out of nowhere and pull us all over. In what seemed like an eternity, I finally spotted the lights of a small town in the near distance. As soon as we entered the town, our pursuer took an abrupt right turn down a dark street and disappeared into the night. We stopped alongside a store in a brightly lit area and composed ourselves while trying to decide whether we should report the incident to the local police. After trying to find some humor in our little adventure, I promised the guys I would not stop driving again until we reached California. Exhausted, I missed the target by sixty miles as we had to spend the next night in Kingman, Arizona.

On the morning of June 22, 1967, we entered the state of California. With our horns blowing, we stopped along the highway just to walk on west coast soil. We even argued about who was the first one to actually set foot in the state. We were experiencing the joy and happiness that people who had scaled the Berlin Wall must have experienced. At last, we were in a place that we had heard and read so much about and where our dreams could possibly come true. Late that afternoon, we arrived in Oakland to spend the night at the home of my Aunt, Evie Lee Flowers.

Early the next morning, thirty-two rookie engineers from colleges and universities all over America reported to the Lockheed Medical Center in Sunnyvale to take physical exams, which were a part of the orientation process. Unaware, I was about to face a new style of racism that was much more subtle than I was accustomed to in the south. A nurse entered the waiting area and asked for Carl Ray to identify himself. I was then informed that prior to taking my physical exam I had to meet with John Edwards, the manager of the Educational Department where new hires were assigned for the first seven months prior to being selected or assigned to a permanent department. I was given a map and directed to a building located about a mile away at the main facility. Upon arriving at his office, I identified myself to his secretary and informed her that Mr. Edwards had requested a meeting with me. Expecting my arrival, Mr. Edwards immediately invited me into his office and proceeded to inform me that he noticed in my file that I was a polio victim and he wanted to know if I felt I would be able to perform the task for which I was being hired. Immediately, I reflected on my training at Tuskegee on how to deal with similar thinking white people. After his inquiry, I didn't hesitate to tell him that I was hired for my mental abilities and not my physical capabilities. I also pointed out to him that only my right hand and arm were affected and I had regained approximately seventy-percent usage of them. I continued by informing him that as an engineer my heaviest tools were pens and pencils and not the shovels and picks used by ditch diggers. In a professional and diplomatic manner, I felt I had given that "white boy" a tongue-lashing, while informing him that I had clearly seen through his bullshit. The old folks at Tuskegee would have been proud of my performance. Upon walking out of his office, I noticed a white employee strolling around in a wheel chair.

Unfortunately, the incident with John Edwards was just a welcome mat in a new world of subtle racism that I would soon learn was imbedded into the fabric of American society. Fortunately we had been taught in the South, racism would look you straight in the face and at the same time stab you in the chest, whereas in other areas of the country, racism would smile in your face and stab you in the back. Knowing that we were playing on an un-leveled field enabled us to design plays to score and succeed in spite of the opposition.

After a month of classes, the new engineers would begin a two-month rotation in three different departments before being assigned to a permanent position. Three of the thirty-two engineers were black and all had Tuskegee connections. Carl Murrell, from Phoenix, Arizona, was the first black engineer to graduate from Arizona State University, but his father had graduated from Tuskegee Institute.

The group was made up of engineers from MIT, Stanford, UC Berkeley, Cal Poly San Luis Obispo and other major universities from across the country, with Tuskegee Institute being the only black college represented. During the departmental introductory meeting, Tuskegee Institute was the only college the manager was not familiar with, even though two of the company's brightest young engineers, Lou Jones and Bill Thaggard, graduated from Tuskegee Institute. Many years later, I would learn that Lockheed was so impressed with their job performances that the company had given a directive to the Personnel department to hire as many engineers from Tuskegee Institute as possible. It was only then that I realized why there were over fifteen engineers from Tuskegee Institute employed with the company in the mid-seventies.

When we began taking classes, I would finally understand why our professors at Tuskegee Institute demanded so much of us. We always thought they were just being overbearing and insensitive with the amount of work and projects that we were assigned. When we questioned them, they would always reply, "When you get out into the world, you are not going to embarrass Tuskegee Institute." Another phrase that was pounded into our subconscious minds was, "You must work twice as hard as your white colleague to be successful."

Our first class was Integrated Circuits-Design Principles and Fabrication. Integrated Circuits (IC's) were the latest state of the art technology and had not been fully implemented in college text books and manuals. During classroom discussion on IC's, TJ and I were the only two engineers who were able to have extended dialogue with the instructor. After class, our fellow engineers began asking us why we knew so much about the subject. With pride, I informed them that the course was just a normal part of the curriculum at Tuskegee. However, I didn't bother telling them that a professor who worked in the industry during the summer would collect as much information on the latest technology that had not been implemented in the textbooks and share that information with us. He always reminded us that the information would enable us to get a head start on our competition when we entered the working world.

My first two assignments would, in a backwards way, contribute to my success and rapid rise in the company. Along with two white classmates, I was assigned to a computer programming department, which was located in a building about a mile from the main facility. The three of us showed up bright and early one morning to meet the department manager and our immediate supervisor. After a brief introduction, the supervisor directed us to his office to discuss our specific assignments. Each of us was given an assignment to write a computer program to perform a series of tests on electrical components. We were given manuals on our individual items and a book on the computer language to be used to write the programs. We were also given a tour of the computer lab, which was located in the main facility and given a brief description and function of the components we were working on. There were ninety-eight people in my department, and I was the only black. I was excited about taking on a new challenge in my life.

The first week was spent reading all of the manuals and books to prepare for the massive task. I took my work home every night, so I could get a head start on my colleagues. I would spend a couple of hours after work in the computer lab talking to anyone that I figured might be an asset in assisting me in the performance of my job. I was so excited about my position that I had failed to notice what was really happening in my own department. My supervisor would only communicate or give me assistance if I went to his office and asked for help. Often I observed him spending time at the two white engineer's desks discussing their projects. At least a couple of times a week he would invite them to lunch. I guess he really didn't see me sitting five feet away from them or maybe he figured I didn't get hungry. I ultimately, decided not to allow his rude and biased behavior to bother me, because I actually wasn't at Lockheed to make friends, even though I was secretly busy building a network of friends and technical people in the main facility to help me with my project. Figuring if no one in my department would talk to me, I might as well use that time to get five steps ahead of them. The unique saying at Tuskegee was, "Always stay five steps ahead of the MAN, in case you slip two steps, you are still three steps ahead."

The main facility where the actual missiles were assembled was like an integrated community with salaried and hourly employees from all ethnic backgrounds working together. Smaller Lockheed facilities located throughout Silicon Valley were staffed with almost one hundred-percent white employees. Even though these facilities were only a few miles from the main facility, the ethnic make-up of the employees was similar to going from the urban area of Los Angeles to Beverly Hills. The cities are twenty miles apart, but a million miles apart, socially, culturally, and other ways.

In an effort to accomplish my goal, my first task was to build my network to connect with all of the black employees in the plant from the janitor to the only two black managers. Since I was receiving only minimum support from my immediate supervision, I had to recruit liberal white engineers, programmers and technicians, who would provide me with the assistance I needed to perform my job adequately. My new network included engineers and programmers who were familiar with the projects that I and my two fellow engineers had been assigned. When they learned which project had been assigned to me, they all had themselves a hearty laugh. Dave, who was one of the coolest white programmers in the company looked at me and smirked, "Son, they gave you the dog's assignment. You're the third young engineer that has gotten stuck with writing a program for this unit. You've been had, my boy! Welcome to the white mans' world." I didn't tell him that I had already been welcomed to the "white mans' world" when I worked for Holiday Inn.

Well, it was time for me to use my people skills. If there was one thing we were taught growing up in the south, it was how to handle white folks and my comic skills would come into play as one of my secret weapons. If you can make people laugh, they will relax, feel comfortable, and give you the shirts off their backs. I truly believe that even though Dave was white, he knew I had been unfairly set up to fail. Because he wanted to stick it to those racists in my department, he was willing to help me. I would always work in my department during the morning and schedule my computer time from eleven to three in the afternoon. This would enable me to have lunch with the engineers and programmers who were always discussing work and problem solving.

In addition to adjusting to my new job, I was searching for an apartment in preparation for the arrival of Jackie and Vicki. However, searching for apartments presented another challenge for me, as I discovered, California wasn't as receptive to blacks as I had expected. Upon arriving to view an apartment, managers of complexes that advertised in newspapers and posted vacancy signs, would politely inform me that the apartment had already been rented and they just had not gotten around to taking down the sign. I was beginning to wonder if I had taken a time machine ride back to Amarillo, Texas. During one occasion, in an effort to verify my suspicion, I disguised my voice while talking on the telephone with an apartment manager so she would not be able to detect that I was black. Upon arrival to the apartment I, once again, were given the old "hadn't taken down the sign routine." After informing her that I had just called from the phone booth less than five minutes earlier and the apartment could not have been rented that quickly, almost instantly her face turned beet red. She went on to claim that she was not the owner and were just following the instructions she had been given.

Eventually, I was able to rent an apartment in nearby Palo Alto. This area, fortunately, turned out to be a perfect location since Jackie would find employment at Stanford University. After calling my friends who were also looking for apartments, the manager rented to them, prompting many of the white residents to complain and move out in protest. Consistent with his ethics, the manager was kind enough to meet with all of the black tenants and assured us that he would continue to rent to any qualified renters, regardless of their race. Prior to us moving in, the complex of seventy apartments had originally maintained approximately a twenty-percent vacancy rate, because they did not previously rent to minorities. This caused the backwards thinking company to lose money.

Now that I had a place to live, I was able to focus more of my time on the job where I was getting my butt kicked with the crappy assignment. The answer to my prayers became a reality one afternoon, when I entered the computer lab and ran into Hank Simon, a black programmer who was sitting at a computer. Hank had graduated from Southern University in Baton Rouge, Louisiana, a historical black college located thirty-five miles from New Roads where I graduated from high school. Because we were both graduates of black colleges, we immediately bonded as if we were relatives. Hank was one of the smartest engineers working for the company and he didn't mind letting people know. On several occasions, white engineers would approach Hank and ask for his assistance when they were having difficultly solving some of their technical problems. Most of the time, he would help them. However, if he was in a bad mood he would simply tell them, "Hell no! If I help you white boys solve your problems, a year from now you'll be the manager and I'll be working for you." Hank was another smart, angry, black man who had his brain power drained too many times, while others reaped the rewards.

Approximately two weeks before I was scheduled to transfer to another department, I had solved the mystery. My program was working! I ran it a couple of times just to be sure before I declared, "Mission Accomplished!" The following morning I excitedly presented my data to my supervisor. Instead of congratulating me for my accomplishment he sarcastically grumbled and said, "Great! This is just what we have been waiting for." Then, along with the two white engineers, he immediately took my test data into the manager's office and proceeded to take all of the credit for solving the problem. Caught somewhere between frustrated and irate, I immediately cleaned out my desk and stormed out of the building, heading back to the Educational Department where I explained the apparent deceit to the manager. Seeing that I wasn't going to receive any satisfaction, I demanded to be assigned to another department.

Once again I realized how cruel and unfair life could be, as I was assigned to another department in the same building and same floor adjacent to my old department. To my amazement, the situation would be much worse than it was in my previous department. My new supervisor was Gary Shultz. I felt the name alone should have been a clue that I was entering into another hornet's nest. The morning I reported to the department, Shultz was in his office talking to a couple of engineers. I introduced myself and informed him that I had been assigned to his group for two months, information he already knew because he had earlier received my transfer requisition. He picked up some drawings off his desk and told me they were for a simulator that wasn't working properly and the unit needed to be redesigned. The only other information I was given was the department, building and the contact person at the main facility where the unit was located. He smugly said, "If you are really an engineer, you should know what to do." He then abruptly turned his back on me and continued his conversation with the two engineers. Wow, my introduction had lasted less than three minutes and I wasn't even given the common courtesy and respect deserving of a professional, nor any technical information about the malfunction of the unit or any other suspected problems. When I walked out of his office, his secretary directed me to my desk, and once again I found myself on my own.

The simulator was located in the same building as the computer lab at the main facility. The first week was spent expanding my network to include engineers and technicians working in my new area. I had already met several of the engineers while working on my previous assignment. Fortunately, Hank was there to cover my back. In addition to being a great programmer, he was also a great design and test engineer. Once again I discovered that I had been assigned a project that would seemingly be impossible for me to complete within two months. But having been taught that I couldn't embarrass Tuskegee, I had made it a mission to prove wrong those attempting to set me up for failure.

Although I wasn't able to solve the problem within my two month rotation, my efforts didn't go un-noticed. Hal Lewis, one of only two black managers in the company, heard about my diligent work ethic and invited me to work in his department during my final rotation. This led me to accepting a permanent position in the department. Carl Murrell would also accept a permanent position in the department. Working for Hal was like a dream come true, as he would become a mentor to both Carl Murrell and me. Out of sixty-seven employees in the department, nine of us were black. Hal had somewhat established an underground railroad for getting blacks into Lockheed, by making prior arrangements with some of his white manager friends. He would recruit blacks into his department, giving them a couple of years experience before transferring them to their departments. As a result of this, Hal was able to by-pass the Personnel Department and hire qualified blacks who would ordinarily not even have been granted a job interview. Due to the large number of blacks working in Hal's department, some of our white colleagues often joked that the department looked like the New York Knicks basketball team, which at the time was uncharacteristically predominantly black.

After working for Lockheed three years, I would, again, realize how well Tuskegee Institute had prepared me to compete and succeed in my profession. Three of the thirty-two engineers who were hired with my group had been promoted to a position that required at least five years of experience with the company. Along with Carl Murrell, I was fortunate to be one of the three. As I ran into my colleagues, they would question how I was able to get promoted to that level without the required experience. With a little rub-it-in-your-face humor, I told them it was because I had attended Tuskegee, implying quietly that I was smarter than those major-school graduates.

Shortly after joining the department, I would be introduced to the sport of bowling by Chuck Gary, a black technician in the department. Chuck started a bowling team which included his wife, Carl Murrell, two white secretaries in the department and me. The bowling league we joined was composed of twenty teams, representing companies, bars, restaurants and organizations throughout Silicon Valley. Our team was groundbreaking, because we were the only integrated team in the league. Because we were one of the few teams without a sponsor, we didn't have flashy shirts and jackets, but I have to admit we had style, which lead to being a little cocky and rowdy. This made a few of the white teams somewhat uncomfortable. When we detected a hint of prejudice from opposing teams refusing to sit in the bowling area and socialize with us, we really turned up the volume. Even some of the best teams would totally collapse while playing against us. It was obvious when they became frustrated, and wanted the games to end, so they could go home and perhaps take a stress pill. Tolerating four "uppity Negroes" and two liberal "white broads" was too arduous for some teams.

Prior to joining the team, I had never bowled; but I quickly mastered the game by practicing four hours every Sunday morning. Chuck, Carl and I would arrive at the bowling alley promptly before the doors opened and helped the manager set up and drink coffee before bowling. As a result of all of the extra practice, my average rose from 140 to 185 within three years.

After a year in California, I had comfortably settled into my new life style. By working for Hal, I no longer had to fight as many sharks on my job and Jackie was working at Stanford University, while Vicki was attending an elementary school two blocks from our apartment. The Bay Area Tuskegee Alumni club introduced us to other Tuskegee alums living in the area as well as other blacks, many who graduated from black colleges. At that time, there were no nightclubs in Silicon Valley that catered to blacks. On the other hand, there were always house parties being held every weekend where good food, plenty of dancing, and card playing lasted until the wee hours of the morning. Yes, California was finally beginning to feel like home.

14
THE DIVORCE

A daily ritual of several of us newly hired engineers was a visit to TJ's, and his roommate, Ellis Jones' apartment after work, where we had a few beers and played cards to unwind from a hard days' work. TJ's younger brother, James, was living with him and Ellis, who were both enjoying the exciting life of bachelorhood. Even though all of his material needs were being met, I felt that James needed to be in a more conventional family atmosphere. In an effort to provide that type of environment I took James home with me for dinner every evening and assisted him with his home work before driving him back home. TJ's apartment was located approximately three miles away in the adjacent city of Mountain View. One night I didn't feel like driving James home so I asked him to spend the night with us and I would take him home the next morning on my way to work. Since we only had a two bedroom apartment James slept on the living room sofa.

The following afternoon I made my usual visit to TJ's after work. When I was leaving for home I noticed that James had his books and a piece of luggage as he approached my car. When I asked why he had the luggage, he replied, "I am going to stay with you." When I arrived home I explained to Jackie that James had decided, without my permission, that he was moving in with us. After a family discussion, which included Vicki, we decided that it would probably be best for him and he could also serve as a big brother to Vicki.

Since we were being adopted by James we needed a three bedroom apartment so that he would have his own bedroom instead of sleeping on the sofa. Fortunately, there was a vacant three bedroom apartment upstairs in the building where we lived. James' payment for moving in was getting three of his friends to help move the heavy items upstairs.

We were excited about James becoming a member of our family. However, we didn't realize that we were about to receive a crash course in being the parents of a teenager. James enrolled in Palo Alto High school, which was located approximately two miles from our apartment. We became his unofficial guardians as we met with his high school counselors, attended PTA meetings and various other school activities. Jackie would drop James off at school on her way to work and pick him up in the afternoon. The school was located just across the street to the entrance of Stanford University where she worked. After a couple of weeks James was walking home after school with his friends or getting rides with their parents.

The transition of James moving in with us had gone smoothly. TJ and I spent so much time visiting each other it was as if James actually had two homes. The new addition to our family temporarily calmed the tension that was brewing in our marriage. In our effort to help James adapt to his new school, the process took the focus away from our problems and of course, we didn't want James to see that we were just another dysfunctional family. The perfect family façade lasted about six months before we resumed our verbal spats and assaults towards each other in his presence. James was now a valid family member so it was okay for him to see who we really were. I think we both realized that even though

James had livened up our home, it was just a matter of time before we would revert back to a fragile marriage that was about to disintegrate before he arrived.

Jackie's drinking got progressively worse and the once verbal confrontations became physical. Disturbing the neighbors in the middle of the night became an embarrassing habit. By the summer of 1969, I knew that divorce was imminent. One night after having a minor disagreement over a petty issue, I went for a calming down walk. When I returned, I took the back stairs and entered the apartment through the kitchen. I was not prepared for what I saw when I opened the door. Jackie stood in the living room, pointing a handgun at me. With little time and even less forethought, I jumped over the railing, landing uninjured eight feet below. I ran a couple of blocks down the street to a phone booth where I called a friend who picked me up and allowed me to spend the night at his apartment.

Jackie pleaded and promised to get counseling for her drinking problem, so after a few weeks, I gave in and moved back home. However, the marriage came to its inevitable end one chilly night in February, 1970. After an evening at a local bar with our friends, Jackie slipped into one of her nasty moods and started a fight with me. Our friends who lived across from our apartment building suggested that I spend the night with them. I accepted their invitation on the condition that they would not let Jackie into their apartment while I was there.

Around four o'clock in the morning I was abruptly awakened by a noise in the hallway. Shortly thereafter someone turned on the light in the bedroom where I was sleeping. I heard Jackie screaming and through sleep ridden eyes, I saw her tussling with my friend as he tried to prevent her from entering the room. Wielding a butcher knife, she cut him during the struggle, prompting him to move out of her way as she entered the bedroom. By that time, I was wide awake but pretended that I was still asleep. As she approached the bed, I strategically rolled out of the way of the knife that she thrust into the mattress. When my friend finally stopped us from fighting, I had defensively hit Jackie in her face several times, blackened one of her eyes and severely bruised her forehead.

After I calmed Jackie down and assured our friends that everything was all right between us, we returned to our apartment. The calming down period was short lived and the realization that everything was not going to be all right was immediately prominent. Hell released its demons as Jackie continued to agitate me. In my frustration, I almost called her a bitch but managed to stop myself before sounding out the last letters. With furious consternation, she asked, "Did you call me a bitch?" Her rage at my apparent infraction increased as she frantically searched for a match to light her cigarette. My suspicion grew when she refused to accept a light from me and instead went into the kitchen to light her cigarette. Suspecting that she was actually heading to the kitchen to get another knife, I quickly followed her. Once in the kitchen, she turned on the stove's burner, lit her cigarette and acted unusually calm, as if everything was fine between us. I was convinced that she was trying to put me at ease so she could retrieve a knife out of the utensil drawer. I pretended to be unaware of her plan, but I silently swore to myself that I would slam the drawer and break her hand before I would allow her to retrieve a weapon. As mentally prepared as I thought I was I was still caught off guard when she quickly opened the drawer, retrieved a knife and slashed my arm in a rapid upward motion. Instinctively, I grabbed her hand before she brought the knife downward in her second attempt to stab me. At that moment, I lost all control. As I hit her repeatedly, I was physically and mentally unable to stop myself. In my brief state of insanity, I saw the life leaving her body and I was overcome with a great feeling of joy, peace and power.

Within seconds, that feeling of power turned to panic as I realized that she was not breathing. I immediately performed my recently learned CPR on her. I performed mouth-to-mouth resuscitation and pumped her chest, but I was unable to restart her heart. After several failed attempts, I slumped on the floor beside her. I felt the joy, peace, and power fade along with my life and my future. A few moments later, I saw her hand suddenly flinch. Immediately, I tilted her head back, cleared her throat and blew air down into her chest as hard as I could. After a couple of puffs, she let out a big breath and began breathing. I felt a faint pulse, but a couple of minutes later, she stopped breathing again. I repeated the process until she started breathing again. Afraid that she might stop breathing again, I refused to leave her side even to call the paramedics until she was able to breathe on her own for at least five minutes. While I waited, I prayed and promised God that if He would let her live, I would never touch her again. When paramedics finally arrived, they quickly transported Jackie to Stanford University Hospital and I followed in my car.

Jackie was released from the hospital around 2 o'clock that Sunday afternoon. Due to her injuries, she was unable to work the following week. She had a patch over one of her eyes, her face and lips were swollen and I was embarrassed and angry at myself because I had allowed myself to be driven to such a low barbaric mental state. Ordinarily, I was not a violent person and I didn't believe in hitting women; but she had pushed me to a breaking point. It disturbed me that even in self-defense I was actually capable of taking the life of another human being. I was blessed that the current domestic violence laws were not enacted during those days, because the paramedics and the hospital emergency room staff would have been required to call the police and I would have been arrested and hauled off to jail.

Even though our relationship was volatile and destructive, we were back together after she was released from the hospital; but one week later I would finally be forced into sanity, prompting me to permanently move out of the apartment. What prompted my return to sanity was a party we attended at our friends' apartment where we had our confrontation the prior weekend. After having just a few drinks, Jackie began telling all of the guests about our unfortunate violent encounter and what she was going to do to me. Even though it was only about 10 p.m., most of the guests decided to leave before we started fighting again. I also decided to leave the party and began walking back to our apartment as Jackie followed. Just as we were about to walk into our apartment, Jackie said that she was going to kill me. Upon hearing those words, I immediately walked to my car that was parked on the street in front of the apartment building. Upon starting the engine, she jumped onto the hood in a futile attempt to stop me from driving away. In another moment of temporary insanity, I revved up the engine and made a U-turn tossing her off the hood onto the street. I didn't even stop to see if she was injured as I drove off, and needless to say, we would never spend another night together.

I immediately filed for a legal separation because I knew in my heart that there would never be any reconciliation of our marriage. I was also naive enough to believe that we could use the same attorney and ease the financial burden on the both of us. However, Jackie absolutely refused to entertain that idea and retained her own attorney. During our first court appearance the judge awarded Jackie the 1967 Ford Fairlane and I was awarded the 1961 Volkswagen

Beetle. The judge also ordered me to pay all of the bills and give Jackie one hundred-fifty dollars a month for housing allowance, which was the monthly rent for her apartment. I knew the judge was being extremely unfair due to the fact that I had produced documents validating the salary she earned at Stanford University, which would have enabled her to at least pay for the rent on her apartment. However, having my freedom and peace of mind back was worth every cent. I continued to pay for the repairs on Jackie's car. However, I was smart enough to keep copies of all of the checks, which proved to be an advantage for me in the final court decision.

In an effort to save our marriage, and at Jackie's request, the judge ordered us to seek help through a marriage counselor. I met Jackie at the counselor's office one afternoon after work. Even though we sat in the lounge of the counselor's office for approximately fifteen minutes before entering his office, we never spoke a single word to each other. When the counselor finally invited us into his office, he attempted to be cordial by offering us a glass of water while chatting about the weather, probably to ease the tension between us. After sharing some background information about his practice he asked each of us to share our feelings about our marriage and if we were in agreement on putting forth the serious effort required to make our marriage work? Jackie spoke first, giving a number of reasons why she felt the marriage could and should be saved. After her well thought out dissertation, the counselor asked me what my thoughts on the reconciliation were. I responded by saying, "The only reason I'm here is because of the court order. There's no way I will ever live with this woman again." He asked if I really felt that way, to which I replied, "Yes." He then turned to Jackie and said, "Mrs. Ray, I don't think we need to proceed any further. I don't think he is going to change his mind." Jackie began to cry uncontrollably as I unconsciously jumped up and walked out of the office.

Once it was obvious that the marriage could not be reconciled, Jackie and her attorney decided to request that I pay alimony and child support even though Vicki was not legally my child. Her attorney even requested that Jackie be awarded a percentage of my projected Lockheed Retirement benefits even though I had only worked three years for the company. Sadly, Jackie didn't realize that I had, in the gambling vernacular, "a couple of aces up my sleeve." One of Jackie's bank statements had been accidently forwarded to my new address. Unconsciously, I open the letter only to discover that her monthly net income was about fifty percent of what my monthly net income was and I was paying all of the bills. And to add insult to injury, Jackie had gone to the Rose Bowl Game in Pasadena, California where Stanford University had played Ohio State University and charged an airline ticket, hotel room, and food to the credit card that the judge had ordered me to pay.

Now the time had arrived to play my aces and put an end to this revolving court room circus. When I met Jackie she said that she was divorced from Vicki's father who lived in San Francisco. She also said that her divorce attorney was Fred Gray who practices law in Tuskegee, Alabama. Attorney Gray was the attorney who represented Rosa Parks during her historic Civil Rights trial for refusing to give up her seat to a white man on a public city bus. Her refusal began the Montgomery Bus boycott. However, reflecting back on a conversation I had overheard between Jackie and her mother about the divorce proceedings caused me to have some doubts about the divorce.

During one of my visits back to Tuskegee I met with Attorney Gray, and explained my situation, and asked if he recalled representing Jackie in her divorce proceedings.

Upon checking his records he found that Jackie had retained him to initiate the divorce but the proceedings were never completed. Attorney Gray, at my request, was kind enough to write me a letter stating what he had told me during our meeting. Armed with that letter, along with her bank statement and my cancelled checks I had the smoking gun I needed to end my marriage nightmare.

During the next court appearance, Jackie and her attorney received a stunning surprise when my attorney requested an annulment of our marriage based on the grounds that Jackie was not divorced from her first husband. The judge asked Jackie to respond to the allegations presented by my attorney. Obviously shaken and almost speechless she managed to blurt out the year and approximate date and the name of her attorney, Fred Gray, who represented her during the divorce proceedings. Upon completion of her statement my attorney presented the letter from Attorney Gray stating that the divorce was never finalized. After carefully reading the letter, the Judge asked Jackie if she could address the issue mentioned in the letter. Jackie looked towards her attorney who remained totally silent as she searched for words to respond to the Judges' request. After slightly composing herself, Jackie said that she thought that… she remembered receiving documents from Attorney Gray indicating the divorce had been finalized. The judge promptly scheduled another court appearance two weeks later at which time Jackie was to present to the court the divorce documents. I walked out of the courtroom thinking that I probably should have shared the letter with Jackie and her attorney in advance, but being that she initiated the war, I was in no mood to assist the enemy.

Exactly two weeks later upon entering the courtroom, I could see defeat written all over Jackie's face. I intentionally wore a smirk of confidence on my face as I stared in the direction of Jackie and her attorney. I felt like I had plunged a jagged edge dagger into her chest and I was enjoying twisting the handle. The judge asked her attorney if they were prepared to present the requested documents, to which he replied, "No your Honor." Based upon his statement and the letter from Attorney Gray, my attorney requested that the judge declare an annulment of the marriage. The Judge not only granted the annulment, he also ordered Jackie to pay fifty percent of the remaining bills that we acquired during our marriage, all of the bills she incurred after the legal separation and I no longer had to pay her the one hundred-fifty dollar monthly maintenance payment. I was finally a free and happy man.

I celebrated my victory by taking a week-long vacation and visiting some of my Tuskegee classmates who lived in Los Angeles. Since this was my first time trip to Los Angeles I was treated to all of the major tourist sites; Universal Studios, Disneyland and the nightclubs in Hollywood. The vacation was the perfect way to close a chapter on a horrible period in my life and begin writing a future that included a happy single life. Unfortunately, I was unaware that another chapter was unfolding in what would seem to be an unending saga.

15
IN-LAWS

Approximately one month after the annulment, I received a phone call from my now X-mother-in-law, Evelyn Smith. Evelyn felt that since I had taken her daughter and granddaughter from Alabama to California, it was my responsibility to pay the expenses to move them to St. Louis, Missouri where she and her husband lived. Even though she told me what I was going to do in a rather harsh tone of voice, I remained calm because I had been taught to respect my elders. I subjected myself to a severe tongue lashing from her for about five minutes as she told me I was a sorry excuse of a man and that she never liked me and she knew her daughter made a mistake when she married me. After several attempts to engage Evelyn in a civilized conversation, it became obvious that being the little Christian boy I was raised to be was not providing any constructive dialogue between us. I tried to talk to her in a civilized, respectful manner, but was constantly interrupted. Once again, I allowed myself to be lowered to an uncharacteristic level of insanity when she threatened to fly to California and physically harm my little body. Upon taking instructions from a little voice in my head, I screamed into the phone, "Bitch, if you come out here ... expletive... with me, I will kick your ass so bad you will fly back to St. Louis without the plane."

Suddenly, there was silence on the other end of the line and I was the one ranting and raving like a maniac. After gaining her attention, and in a non-Christian manner, I told her what part of my anatomy she could kiss as I slammed the phone down. I felt a tiny bit of shame for a few seconds as I thought of Momma, knowing that she wouldn't approve of such behavior. However, Momma probably never expected that there would be some foul-mouth old woman talking to her baby boy in such an inappropriate manner. Honestly, I really enjoyed slamming that old witch.

Three weeks later my manager rushed into my cubicle and asked if he could see me in his office. The urgency in his voice and the paleness of his appearance made me wonder if he had seen a ghost. Rapidly closing the door as we entered his office, he informed me that he had just received a phone call from a gentleman named Melvin Smith who said he was my father-in-law. He said that Mr. Smith was in California and he was demanding that Lockheed force me to pay all of the expenses to have his daughter moved to St. Louis. He explained to Mr. Smith that the company did not get involved in their employees personal affairs. However, it appeared that Mr. Smith did not understand and threatened to sue the company if his demands were not met. I assured my manager that I would handle the matter and that he would receive no more calls from Mr. Smith.

When I arrived home from work, I called Jackie and learned that Evelyn and Melvin had arrived in California the night before. During my conversation with Jackie, Melvin picked up the other phone and informed me of the conversation he had with my manager that afternoon. He also voiced his opinion on me disrespecting Evelyn during my prior conversation with her. Melvin continued by telling me that if I didn't pay to move Jackie and Vicki back to St. Louis he would have to take care of me. He bragged that he was a former street hustler from the Ghetto and he knew how to make people disappear.

"Is that a threat?" I asked.

Sarcastically, he replied, "You are a smart Nigger. You figure it out!"

For the third time, I felt forced to step outside of my Christian upbringing and verbally assaulted that old useless wannabe gangster. The heated verbal battle lasted about three minutes as we made all kinds of profane promises to eliminate each other. Shortly after hanging up the phone, I realized that once again I had allowed another member of that family to bring out the beast in me and I was ready to take a human life.

Weeks passed without any communication from Jackie and her family. Then, early one morning I was awakened from a deep sleep by what I considered to be a prank call. An anonymous female voice announced, "You are dead! There is a hit out on you!" I didn't think the call was a serious threat so I rolled over and went back to sleep. The next morning I received an unsettling phone call from James Johnson, who once lived with Jackie and me. He warned me to be careful because Evelyn and Melvin had really put a contract out on me. I didn't take him too seriously until he told me that they had paid one of Jackie's friends, Barbara Thompson, fifty dollars to hire someone from East Palo Alto to kill me. According to him, Barbara had given some guy two-hundred dollars to do the job. East Palo Alto was a predominantly black neighborhood located on the southern end of the San Francisco Bay where drugs and gang violence was just beginning to flourish and anything could be purchased there for a few dollars.

Once James mentioned Barbara's name, I knew that the threat was legitimate. I had witnessed Barbara's insanity first hand one night at a local bar where she had accompanied

Jackie and me for drinks. A black male and a Hispanic male, neither of whom we knew, started fighting. As we exited the bar along with the other patrons, Barbara reached into her purse, pulled out a gun and attempted to pass it to the black male. Fortunately, I retrieved the gun from her hand just before the exchange was made. Once we were in the car, I asked her why she'd attempted to give a gun to some guy that she didn't even know. She replied, "So he could kill the S.O.B." After that evening I never again went anyplace with Barbara although she and Jackie remained friends or at least drinking buddies.

After I received the call from James, I immediately left work in search of another apartment. I found a one bedroom furnished apartment in a complex approximately one mile from where my apartment was located. The apartment building was located on a narrow street in a predominately white neighborhood in Sunnyvale, California. The street had very few trees and was well lit at night which made it easy to spot a black male who might be parked or driving in the area. After the manager showed me the apartment, I asked when it might be possible for me to move in. I sighed with relief when he said, "Anytime you want too." Since I didn't want to spend another night in my apartment, I had stopped by my credit union to withdraw enough cash to pay the deposit and first month's rent. I explained to the manager that I needed to move a few boxes in that night because my roommate's girlfriend and her two children had suddenly moved in with us and I needed my own space. My little fabrication had caused the manager to hear my urgent plea and he said I could move in that night. Prior to going back to work I went to my apartment to get a few of my belongings. I carefully surveyed the area. I drove past the apartment three times, observed all of the parked cars, and looked for any suspicious characters. After careful surveillance, I parked in the rear of the complex. I sneaked through a side gate into my apartment and loaded as many items as I could get in approximately twenty minutes. The first item I retrieved was my gun which I planted firmly in my hand during each trip I made to my car. I felt like I was in a scene from a gangster movie, except my fear was real.

After moving into my new apartment I completely changed my pattern of movement for my protection. I took different streets to work each day and parked in a parking lot near the rear of the complex, which meant I had to walk approximately one-quarter mile to my office building. There was several security gates located around the perimeter of the Lockheed complex, which spanned an area approximately three-quarters of a mile by one-half mile. Employees had to present identification badges to enter the facility and once inside I was safe. My office was located in a huge two-story building approximately two-hundred yards long and seventy-yards wide. Because of the classified work performed in the building, there were no windows.

As an extra safety precaution I remained at work for two or three hours each day after the shift ended. This circumstantial, self-imposed extension didn't go unnoticed by my manager. On several occasions he complimented me on the extra hours I spent on the job even though I wasn't getting paid. The extra time allowed me to complete most of my assigned projects ahead of schedule, which led to my manager giving me high ratings on my performance reviews for which I was rewarded handsomely through a promotion and salary increase. I never felt the need to share with him why I was really so dedicated to my work even though I felt a little guilty about all of the accolades I received for my work ethics. However, my guilt wasn't great enough to cause me to turn down the promotion and increase in my salary. I am told somewhere in the Bible it is written, "What some intended for bad, God intended it for good." Therefore, the advancement on the job was actually the work of a Higher Being.

I continued the cloak and dagger routine for about eight months. After that length of time I assumed the guy probably had spent almost two-hundred in gas just looking for me and hopefully had given up. I'm exceedingly grateful that he never fulfilled his end of the contract. However, if I had not received a warning from James… well I prefer not to think about what might have happened. James was just another angel carrying out his assignment from God. James graduated from high school and worked for Lockheed in the same building where I worked. He remained with the company until he retired.

Jackie and Vicki moved to St. Louis, Missouri to live with Evelyn and Melvin. Although I wouldn't have any communication with Jackie for the next three years, I would periodically write letters to Vicki even though I never received any response back from her. I had grown attached to her and thought of her as my own child. My intuition told me that Evelyn was intercepting the letters but I would continue to write her. Approximately five years later I received a letter from Evelyn. I carefully opened the letter as if I expected a letter bomb and was even more surprised as I read the contents. Evelyn was actually apologizing for her negative behavior towards me during my marriage and divorce from Jackie. She stated that she had kept Vicki from communicating with me and realized how much she was hurting her. Evelyn also said that she had come to realize that I was the only father that Vicki had ever known and it was obvious that she needed a positive figure in her life due to the fact the Jackie had a serious drinking problem. I was even more surprised when she asked if I could find it in my heart to forgive her for the way she had treated me. She said that she had accepted the fact that Jackie had some serious emotional problems and she understood why I divorced her and she would allow Vicki to visit me if I still wanted to see her.

After reading the letter I knew that I had to forgive her. If Evelyn was woman enough to write me a ten page letter asking forgiveness for her misdeeds against me I had no choice but to forgive her. By releasing her through forgiveness we were both set free. As time passed, we developed a close relationship and I visited Evelyn and Melvin in St. Louis even though I must admit that my first visit was a little uncomfortable.

Even though I had gone through a bitter divorce process, I felt it was worth all of the heartache, energy and money just to have some peace in my life. I was still taking classes at San Jose State University, but for the first time I began to question myself about what I was really doing with my life. For the first time I realized that most of the choices I had made in my life were actually made by someone else. I attended college because of Daddy's house rule, "You are not grown until you get a college degree." I do believe it was one of his greatest rules he imposed upon me and my siblings for which I will be ever grateful. Further, I found myself in graduate school only because the policy of the company dictated that a technical degree combined with an MBA was the path to upper management. My personal battle was that, I didn't really know what I wanted to do with my life that would make me happy. Without trying to come to a quick decision, I decided to give myself a few months to figure out what was my true life's purpose.

After about three months of brainstorming, I came up with the career that I really felt in my heart that I wanted to pursue. Entertainment! My choices were a singer or comedian, even though I had no idea of how or where to begin. My only experience in either area was performing at talent shows in high school. My first step was to enroll in a voice class at a local community college and I began checking out a couple of bands that I could possibly join. Of course I didn't share my new found goals with anyone for fear of being run out of town for even considering such a crazy idea of giving up a budding engineering career for an uncertain try at entertainment. My career choice would summon me even more when I heard a radio advertisement about a comedy class at a local theater in San Francisco. Being that comedy was one of my career choices I saw this as a sign from the Almighty.

16
THE BEGINNING OF MY COMEDY CAREER

After work I drove to the Intersection Theater in San Francisco and met Frank Kidder, the instructor, and his comedy partner Bob Barry. The class was held in a room in the basement of the theater which also served as a comedy club during weekends. The room was dimly lit with a twelve inch riser which served as the stage surrounded by a few worn tables and chairs. The rear of the room was occupied with a couple of stained sofas.

By the time class began, eight other eagerly excited guys had arrived. Throughout the class Frank and Bob would take turns discussing the pros and cons of stand-up comedy. They explained that the first step to becoming a successful comedian was learning how to write a joke. The second step was to paint the premise; and the third step, was to deliver the punch line. Premise and punch line were my first official introduction to comedy language. The first assignment for each student was to stand before the class and tell any joke they knew. Afterwards, there was a ten minute break in which each person had to write a joke and present it to the class which would be critiqued by Frank and Bob. Members of the class were also invited to make comments or suggestions about each other's newly written material.

After the two week class, during which time each comic had written, practiced and honed his five-minute routine, it was time to showcase before a real live audience. Instead of allowing comedians to have their first performance at the Intersection Theater where classes were held and comics would have been more comfortable, Frank held the first showcase at the less popular Spaghetti Factory. Once Frank felt that a comic had achieved some success with the audiences at the Spaghetti Factory, the comic would be allowed to perform at the Intersection Theater. The Spaghetti Factory or "Hell Hole" as I referred to it was located in the North Beach section of the City. There was a dingy, poorly lit room in the back of the building with a small stage and a bright spotlight hanging from the ceiling about twenty feet from the stage. Most of the people in the audience were usually drug users or lost souls down on their luck and looking for a place to come in out of the bad weather. Some would even lay with their heads on the tables, fast asleep; while other people were having their private conversations, oblivious of the comics who graced the stage just a few feet away. The real entertainers were the hecklers who received cheers and applause whenever they were successful at running a comic off stage before completing his routine.

I was almost overtaken by fear when I arrived at the Spaghetti Factory for my showcase and observed all of the people hanging out on the street. Among the crowd were, Hell's Angels milling around their bikes drinking beer and smoking marijuana. There were also winos, prostitutes and what appeared to be a couple of guys selling drugs. I had made the mistake of arriving an hour before the showcase began. I spent my time at the bar drinking cokes and pretending to read a borrowed newspaper, which enabled me to avoid making eye-to-eye contact with anyone. After what seemed like an eternity, Frank and several comics arrived

151

about five minutes before showcase began. However, Frank would leave after introducing us to the MC who had the responsibility of overseeing us, critiquing our performance and reporting back to Frank our progress. Based upon the MC's evaluation, Frank would determine when a comic could be promoted to the Intersection Theater. After spending an hour around those weirdoes while waiting for Frank to arrive, my goal was to impress the MC enough so he would give a favorable report to Frank and I would not have to come back to the Spaghetti Factory.

The MC was a tall, bleach-blond surfer guy named Tyler Horn. The order in which the comics would appear on stage was determined by drawing numbers out of a beer mug. The prayer of each comic was not to pull the number "one" because the first comic on stage was ultimately like a sacrificial lamb to be thrown into a fiery pit. Everyone knew when a comic drew the first slot by the groan he would emit as if someone pierced his heart with a jagged dagger. Luckily my prayer was answered when I selected the number, "seven." The chants and boos from the audience began as soon as Tyler walked onto the stage... "Get off stage!" "You ain't funny!" And, their favorite phrase, "you suck!" Of course the chants from the audience didn't appear to bother Tyler who appeared to be more interested in showing off his almost perfectly built tanned body than he was in getting laughs.

Oddly, the best comics of the night were three male hecklers, a black, white and Hispanic, who occupied the table located directly in front of the stage. I soon referred to them as the "Affirmative Action hecklers." Each time they were able to encourage a comic to abandon or give up his/her routine and walk off stage, they would stand, turn around and face the audience with raised hands as they received laughs and applause. As I sat in the back of the club nervously watching the comics who went up on stage before me, I came up with a unique plan to win the hecklers over to my side.

When I went up on stage, I focused attention on the hecklers by asking the audience to give them a hand for being so funny and I spent my entire time on stage playing to them, not once looking at anyone else in the audience. My five minute routine that I had practice several times in class lasted only about three minutes with no pauses at the end of jokes for laughter. My focus of putting them in the spotlight and recognizing their talent as hecklers worked far beyond my expectations. When I finished my routine, the three of them got up on stage and raise my hand as if I was a prize fighter and declared me the winner and the audience gave me a big round of applauds just as they directed them to do. Tyler gave a thumb's up report to Frank and the following week I was rewarded with a slot at the Intersection Theater.

Eventually, I became so consumed in my new found career that I would drive over fifty miles to San Francisco five nights every week and hang out at coffee houses and bars just for the opportunity of getting five minutes on stage. Several nights when I finally was able to get some stage time, it was after midnight and most of the audience had petered out and vacated the building. I would usually arrive home around 2 a.m. in the morning, crawl in bed totally exhausted, and then would be in my work office by 7 a.m., only to begin the daily routine all over again.

Miraculously, God sent me the shield of comedy to protect me from the demons that had opened up an all-out assault on me. I was dealing with the stress of a nasty divorce and the stigma of dropping out of the MBA program at San Jose State University. God also slipped one of His greatest angels into my life in the form of a blind date. Friends introduced me to Brenda Smith, an attractive intelligent Afro-Centric young lady with an exceptional cute three year old son, Ejalu. However, I explained to her that I was too engrossed in my new found career and that I really didn't have time for dating. She was working a full time job, going to graduate school, and active in the community; she was not fazed by my sincere and seemingly self-absorbed assertion. After a thirty minute conversation and kiss, I went on my merry way, oblivious to the fact that she would become my wife a few years later.

On a rainy night in February, 1973, I was leaving for my nightly drive to San Francisco when I received a call from my brother, Lemarvin. He informed me that Bill Carlisle, my father's killer, had been shot and killed by his wife's father. According to reports, Bill was beating his wife, Clara, when her father intervened. Even though Clara's father had his gun drawn, Bill attacked him. In a futile effort to stop her father from shooting Bill, Clara stepped between them. She sustained a gaping wound to her hand as the bullet that passed through it struck Bill in the face, killing him instantly.

I reminisced how Bill's in-laws had been supportive of him after he killed Daddy. They actually posted a five-thousand dollar bond for Bill's release from jail. In a morbid twist of irony, Bill had shown his gratitude by forcing his father-in-law to kill him. The families of Bill and his wife conspired with the lawyers and the court to keep Bill from serving any prison time for the pre-meditated murder of Daddy. Their reward for being his temporary refuge was to become his executioners. Although I would not wish for anyone, not even the Carlisle family, to experience such a tragedy, I will concede that I couldn't help thinking that Hollywood could not have written a better script to depict the demise of Bill Carlisle's life.

Upon hearing the news, I was simultaneously saddened and enraged. Saddened because I had lost the object of my hatred and enraged because I felt God had allowed Bill Carlisle to escape this life without proper punishment for his transgressions. The first thought that entered my mind was, "God, I don't have anybody else to hate." I had always visualized Bill suffering from an incurable disease and experiencing years of excruciating pain before dying a slow death. I wanted him to experience a pain comparable to, if not greater than, the pain and suffering he had imposed on my family. I wanted him to experience the wrath of hell on this side of life in case he ended up in heaven through some divine loop hole of which I was not aware.

After talking to Lemarvin that night, I lost my appetite for making people laugh, but I drove to the city and watched the other comics perform their routines.

A year after enrolling in the comedy class, I had become a legitimate member of the San Francisco comedy scene. Frank's core group of comedians was performing at all of the new comedy venues throughout the Bay Area. One of his top students was a zany kid named Robin Williams, who would rise to stardom as Mork in the television sitcom, "Mork and Mindy," and later attain iconic status in the world of comedy and motion pictures. Even though there were very seldom any paid gigs, just getting the experience performing before an audience was worth more than money. In reality, most of us would have paid a few bucks for the opportunity. Whenever Frank could charge a few dollars for us performing he said, "Fellas, the money ain't great, but you are getting quality stage time."

In an effort to gain more stage time, we were constantly soliciting owners of bars and cafes to allow us to have open mike nights where comics would be able to perform. Since the owners didn't have to pay the comics and the open mikes were on their slowest business nights, it was a win-win situation for both parties.

I convinced the owner of the Living Room night club in Milpitas where I lived to let me host a comedy night and I even got him to agree to pay the comics if a minimum of thirty people attended the show. Since I lived and worked in the area and a couple of articles about me performing comedy had been written in the local papers, I considered myself a local celebrity. I knew that I could beg at least thirty people from Lockheed to attend the show. I was one of only a few comics who lived in the Silicon Valley and I had built up a small following by performing at parties sponsored by sororities, fraternities, and social clubs. My next job was convincing the comics to drive fifty miles from the city to perform at the club. The distance was not what frightened them. Instead, it was that the Living Room was a predominately black nightclub. The thought of being in a club with more than four black people made the hair on their heads stand up and I really had to use a sales pitch to get them to even consider performing. I finally had to dig deep into my bag of tricks to convince those white boys that the audience would be a group of highly educated and professional blacks that worked in companies and taught at schools in Silicon Valley.

I was finally able to book three comedians, including Robin Williams for my opening night. My original plans were to MC the show, introduce the comics, and perform a few minutes between each act. On the opening night of the show, a meeting was held in the parking lot and the comics requested a slight change in the order of the show. Due to their fear of playing before a black audience they suggested that I open and close the show so that by the time the show ended they would be well on their way back to the city. So I changed the line up from Robin Williams being the last comic to perform, to the opening act, since he had great improvisational skills that enabled him to adapt to almost any type of audience. The best part of the evening for me was watching those panic-stricken comics pace around the parking lot drinking beer, smoking and trying to settle their nerves as they observed the mostly black patrons file into the club. I could relate to what they were feeling as it reminded me of my first night performing to the all white crowd at the Spaghetti Factory.

I opened the show to a packed house with about ten white people including my supervisor and friends from Lockheed. My work associates were unaware that they were part of my White Affirmative Action Program to keep the white comics from filing a discrimination lawsuit against the club. After warming up the crowd for about ten minutes, I introduced Robin. And in keeping with the black audience tradition, there were several wannabe comics in the audience and as soon as Robin walked on stage there was a comment heard from a brother in the crowd. Instantly, Robin switched into his black dialect and began to talk about the brothers' ancestors. The audience went wild and he had them eating out of his hands for the entire time he was on stage. Hearing the sounds of laughter coming from inside the club, the comics rushed inside to watch Robin work his magic. Afterwards, every comic relaxed and ended up having a great set! After the show the comics didn't rush back to the city. They actually hung out and mingled with the audience. For those comics to be able to perform and be funny before a predominately black audience was like a gunfighter winning a shootout in the "Old Wild West."

On the financial arrangements, the owner would pay Robin fifteen dollars and ten dollars to the other comics and I would receive thirty dollars for booking and hosting the show. After I spoke with the owner, he readily agreed that

Robin deserved at least twenty-five dollars for his brilliant performance. In spite of the slight raise, even to this day, I still have the dubious distinction and bragging rights of earning more money than Robin Williams. Well… at least for that one night.

By 1975, I was beginning to consider the possibility of leaving engineering and taking a chance on my dream of becoming a professional comedian. My dilemma was how to make that choice since life after the divorce was going great for me on and off the job. Because I was being promoted every couple of years, my salary increased every six to twelve months. I also owned a house, two cars, and was receiving great medical benefits. I was faced with the difficult choice of giving up my comfortable life style for my dream of becoming a comedian, which might take several years before I would be able to earn enough money for me to meet my basic needs. There were no guarantees that I would ever be successful as a comedian. Choosing a career in entertainment wasn't like enrolling in college where you studied for four or five years, obtained a degree and some company would hire you with a great starting salary.

In addition to figuring out how to make the transition from engineering to comedy, I was faced with the fact of maintaining a distance relationship with my future wife, Brenda, who I had been dating. Although marriage was not in our immediate or distant plans at that time, we decided to build a house on a lot she had purchased in the east foothills of San Jose. Since I was going to sell my house, I reasoned building a house together might work as a business deal, a partnership.

17
CHANGING CAREERS

In the summer of 1976, I made plans to leave Lockheed and move to Hollywood. My plans, and those of several other comics, had been put on the fast track due to the instant success of Robin becoming a cast member on the upcoming re-make of the Rowan and Martin's "Laugh In Comedy Show." George Schlatter, the executive producer of the show, held auditions in Chicago and New York to select the remaining members of the cast. Robin convinced George to come to San Francisco in his search for cast members.

Approximately twenty comedians were selected to perform a five minute audition for George and his staff at the Holy City Zoo Comedy Club in San Francisco. Auditioning for the renowned Hollywood television producer was the most exciting moment most of us had experienced in our short part-time comedy careers. I was fortunate enough to be one of the comics selected to audition. The other hopefuls and I had been encouraged to spend the week prior to the audition practicing and rehearsing the best five minutes of our material for the audition.

On the night of the audition, comics arrived at the club two hours early. The evening was a festive occasion. Some of the comics wore bright colored shirts, vests, ties, and jackets to set themselves apart from the other comics and hopefully to leave a memorable impression in the minds of George and his staff members. Jubilation filled the atmosphere as we prepared to get our first real taste of show business. We milled around outside the club watching the overflow of patrons file in. The show actually began outside the club as comics, in an effort to burn off some of their nervous energy, told jokes and tried out some of their comedy lines on unsuspecting patrons entering the club.

The small club was jam-packed with patrons, including family members and friends who had been recruited by the comics. Before the audition began, George dawn the stage and thanked the comics for accepting the invitation to showcase for him. In reality he probably knew every comic was grateful and most would have paid his travel expenses just to have the opportunity to grace the stage in his presence. George concluded his pep talk with the customary pulling of numbers to determine the order in which comics would appear on stage. Once again the angels watched over me as I drew number nine. However, just getting the opportunity to audition was far more important than the time slot.

After the audition George applauded us by saying he had just witnessed the most amazing group of talented comics. We realized that he probably gave the same speech after every audition, but it made us feel really special. George informed us that he and his staff would complete their review of each comic and let us know their decision within a week. He also said that there were several comics that he would like to call back for a second audition. The following week was filled with anticipation as each of us waited for a call. Finally, by the end of the week nine comics were chosen for the second audition and I was one of them.

The second audition was more stressful than the first because we had already performed our best five minutes of material. Even more stress was added by the rumor that only two spots remained to be filled on the show. On the night of the second audition, the lively festive, joking atmosphere surrounding the first audition was replaced with a more subdued mood as comics isolated themselves in their cars or the coffee shop adjacent to the club to focus on their notes or just mediate.

The greatest performance of the evening was delivered by comic Jim Giovanni, a gifted impersonator that enthralled audiences with his almost perfect impressions of Bill Cosby, John Wayne, Sergeant Bilko, Lucille Ball and other renowned personalities. Jim controlled the audience from the moment he appeared on stage as Peter Falk's character, Lieutenant Columbo, the superficial, absentminded homicide detective who practiced unusual methods of solving murder crimes. Jim, dressed in the character's signature wrinkled trench coat and black necktie, dangled a cigar between his fingers as he mimicked every Columbo body movement to perfection. He stumbled about the stage for approximately thirty seconds before uttering a single word as the audience roared with laughter. When Jim finally spoke in the exact voice of the character, he mesmerized the audience. They gave him a standing ovation as he left the stage. Even George and his staff were standing. Auditioning after Jim's performance was synonymous to eating left-over's. Jim had sucked up almost all of the laughs in the club.

One week after the second audition, Jim Giovanni and Bill Rafferty were chosen as cast members on the "New Laugh In Comedy Show." We all glowed with excitement as if we were all going to be on the show. Even more importantly, three comics from San Francisco were members on the show. San Francisco had become a legitimate comedy Mecca as comics from around the Country began moving to the Bay Area to hone their comedic skills before moving on to Hollywood.

Having been caught up in all of the comedy hoopla, I resigned from Lockheed in November of 1976, but remained in the area until May of 1977. I made several visits to Hollywood to check out the comedy scene while surveying neighborhoods where I might wish to live.

Prior to my move, on April 3, 1977, God blessed me with another angel, my daughter Amelia. Who eventually followed in my footsteps and became an entertainer. She travels the world performing as a singer and musician. Amelia's mother, Donnie Turner, and I were friends and co-workers at Lockheed.

My house in Milpitas, California sold in May, 1977. I rented an unfurnished apartment in Hollywood on Bronson Avenue just one-half block north of Hollywood Boulevard. The apartment was located on a quiet street with tall palm trees nestled at the base of the Hollywood Hills beneath the famous Hollywood Hills sign perched high up on the hillside overlooking the Los Angeles basin. I borrowed a truck from a friend and moved only enough furniture to fill my one-bedroom apartment. I sold most of my appliances and extra furniture at a garage sale and donated what was left to Goodwill.

Upon arrival in Hollywood, I was amazed to see the number of comics who were at the comedy clubs each night. By the end of summer at least a couple hundred new faces were on the scene, including newly emerging comediennes. Most of us were in awe of being in Hollywood. My comic friends from the Bay Area and I spent the first few weeks getting acquainted with the area. We casually strolled the streets of Hollywood, pointing out buildings and store fronts and naming the movies or television shows that were filmed at those locations. As we walked along Hollywood's

Walk of Fame, we had contests to see who could name the movies or television shows in which particular stars had appeared. There were several small cafés with patios at street level where we would spend our afternoons sipping sodas, writing jokes and watching people. Actually, we did more people watching than joke writing. The cafes were usually packed with aspiring entertainers discussing the business and networking to jumpstart their careers. Listening to the constant buzz of chatter from the patrons was like listening to a symphony orchestra.

Occasionally, we glimpsed a movie star cruising by in an expensive car, which in our own minds validated us as potential stars just by being in the area. Later, in a casual conversation with friends we might mention that we saw Clint Eastwood or whoever the star might have been, without giving any details under which the brief sightings occurred.

The evening hours were spent hanging out and watching the endless stream of comics performing their five to ten minute comedy routines at the Comedy Store on Sunset Boulevard, the Improv Comedy Club on Melrose Avenue and other comedy clubs in the vicinity. Within a few short weeks we were getting onto the same stages as we launched the second phase of our careers and we were just as excited as any group of freshmen entering high school. My excitement of being in Hollywood was juxtaposed with my plans of building a house back in San Jose. Construction on the house began in July of 1977 and was to be completed in December of that year. However, there were constant delays which required me to make unscheduled trips back to San Jose. These frequent trips were rapidly depleting my savings.

Brenda finally moved into the house in June of 1978 which meant that in order for me to help with the cost of maintaining the house I needed to earn more money. I had been scanning the want ads and knew there were lots of engineering positions available. By the summer of 1978, I had exhausted most of my savings and was in search of a full-time job. I was working as a part-time telephone salesman but wasn't making enough money to support myself. I never really felt comfortable trying to sell people things that they didn't want, need, and in some cases, couldn't afford.

One morning I picked up a newspaper and saw an ad for a Quality Assurance Engineer at Ed Cliff Industries in Monrovia, about twenty-five miles east of Hollywood. Even though I was not a Quality Assurance Engineer, I knew what the job entailed because Quality Assurance Engineers were always assigned to oversee projects that I had worked on at Lockheed.

I dusted off my portable typewriter and quickly prepared a resume before calling the company to inquire about the position. After a brief conversation with the personnel director about my qualifications and experience with Lockheed, I was granted an interview. On the morning of the interview, I arrived in a suit and tie that I had not worn for two years. Edcliff Industries was located in a two story building in an Industrial Park just west of the Interstate and employed approximately one hundred and twenty people. Edcliff Industries was a far cry from the mammoth Lockheed Missiles and Space Company which at one time employed almost thirty-thousand people in its Silicon Valley facility.

Upon arriving at the company, I was greeted by the personnel director, a tall attractive African American woman, who invited me into her office and offered me a cup of coffee. After a brief conversation, she escorted me to meet Bill Bumstead, the manager of the QA Department and the person I would be working for if I was hired for the position. In his late fifties or early sixties, Bill was a short, slightly over-weight white guy with a pot belly and gray hair. Impressed with my qualifications, Bill was also curious about my two year hiatus from the industry. Without giving him the complete story, I told him about my venture into the entertainment industry. I explained that since the business suddenly had taken a slight downturn I was reviving my engineering career.

After reviewing my resume and giving me a description of the job requirements for which I was being interviewed, Bill gave me a tour of the facility. The upstairs level housed the department managers, engineers and draftsmen; the technicians and assembly line workers occupied the first level. After the tour, Bill assigned one of the design engineers to entertain me while he returned to his office to tend to some urgent matters. However, I would learn later that Bill had gone to have a chat with the personnel director and encouraged her to persuade me to accept the position.

When I returned to the personnel director's office, I was informed that Bill was impressed by my qualifications and he was sure that I was the man for the job. She asked if I was interested in the position, and if so, when would I be available to begin working. I informed her that I had an interview scheduled with another company the following day and would let her know my decision within a week. Without hesitation, she put all of her cards on the table when she asked, "What salary range and type of benefits are you looking for and if the company could meet your demands, would you accept the position?" Not wanting to seem over anxious, I took a moment to think about what she had just offered and realized that I had the upper hand. Leaving some room to negotiate, I gave her a salary figure approximately twenty-five percent higher than what I expected to receive. She excused herself, obviously to discuss my proposition with Bill. Before the interview I hadn't expected to be in a position to name my own salary. The most I had expected was that I would be told how much the salary would be and I would either accept or reject the offer. Approximately five minutes later, she returned to the office and informed me that if I could begin work the following day, they would pay me the salary I had requested. She said she understood that since I was no longer looking for employment, I would have to cancel my interview with the other company. That, I assured her, wouldn't be a problem. While trying to maintain my composure, I acted if I wasn't overly excited about accepting the position. With a firm hand shake she told me that she would have all of the necessary paperwork for me to sign when I reported for work the following day.

I managed to calmly get into my car and drive out of the parking lot before letting out a big scream, "YES! I will have a paycheck coming in two weeks!" God had come through with flying colors! Not only did I get the job, but I would also be earning a higher salary than I expected.

Once again I was spending my days at a full time job and spending my nights in the comedy clubs. The major difference was that I lived within a ten-mile radius of most of the clubs. I had left San Francisco where I was a big fish in a small pond and ended up in Hollywood where I was a small fish in an ocean. Getting quality stage time would be difficult due to the large number of aspiring comics in Hollywood.

The following two years would be nothing more than a blur as I worked five days per week and flew or drove back to San Jose twice a month. To reduce my monthly expenses, I moved in with my friend David Varner who owned a home in South Central Los Angeles. Prior to moving to Los Angeles, I had met and become close to David and his family. Because of my work schedule, I was spending less time on my comedy career. I was at the crossroads of my life and I had to make a career choice between being an engineer or a comedian. I knew that I would never achieve any real success as a comedian while working a full time job because comedy required almost one-hundred percent of one's time.

Brenda suggested that I pick a date that I wanted to resign from my job and leave on that date regardless of finances. She encouraged pursuit of my comedy career to get it out of my system because she didn't want me at sixty-five years of age talking about what I could have done. I selected the date of my resignation by closing my eyes and flipping through the pages of a calendar. When I opened my eyes, I had my finger on July 10, 1980. Exactly two weeks prior to that date, I walked into Bill's office and gave him my resignation letter. Bill wasn't surprised because he knew about my interest in comedy. We had discussed it on several occasions. Actually, he and a couple of the engineers had come to the Laugh Factory Comedy Club in Hollywood to see one of my performances.

18
TAXI DRIVER

After resigning from Edcliff, I realized I needed to find a part-time job to earn enough money to pay my basic living expenses. I didn't have a preference for a specific type of work; I just knew I wasn't good at selling. I discovered the answer to my job situation at Mr. Woodley's Blues club in South Central Los Angeles, where singers and comics showcased their talent every Tuesday night. When fellow comedian Hank Newsome drove up in a taxi, I asked why he was driving a taxi, to which he replied, "Man, this is my side hustle." Hank said he made enough money driving three days a week to take care of his financial needs and have more than enough time to hit all of the local comedy clubs. I asked him what were the requirements for driving a taxi and did he think I could get hired by the company where he worked? He said all I needed was a driver's license and a good driving record. There were always openings because most of the drivers were comics or actors and they were always leaving when they got a comedy gig, television or movie work. Hank gave me the address of the company and told me to meet him the following day and he would introduce me to the owner. He told me that I probably should not tell the owner I was a comedian because comedians had a reputation for leaving the job without giving a notice.

The next day I met Hank during his lunch break at the

Celebrity Cab Company located on South La Brea Avenue. He invited me upstairs to meet the owner who was yelling at some poor cabbie telling him how stupid he was. Then he looked at Hank and in the same loud voice asked, "What the hell do you want?" Hank, seemingly unfazed by his tone of voice said, "This is my friend, Carl Ray. He's interested in driving for you." The owner, Vince De Luca, was a true Italian in every sense of the word. My first impression was that I should turn and run for the door but before I could respond, he pointed to his office and told me to go in and have a seat. He then turned his attention to the dispatchers and started cursing at them. I could see that he probably wouldn't hire me. I was not comfortable lying, so I decided to tell him the truth. During the interview, I explained to him that I was pursuing a comedy career and there would be occasions when I would have to travel out of town for a couple of weeks. However, I would love to continue driving when I returned. Vince said he really appreciated me being honest and he would help me anyway he could. He pointed to some photos on his office wall of former drivers who had become successful in the entertainment business. It was obvious that Vince was as proud of them as if they were his children.

After a short interview, Vince gave me a form indicating that I had been hired by his company and instructed me to carry it downtown Los Angeles to the Department of Transportation. I paid a forty-dollar fee for my taxi permit and photo which had to be displayed in the cab whenever I was working. The following morning I was assigned to ride with an experienced cabby for four hours while he gave me a crash course on reading my map book so I could locate potential customer's addresses in a timely manner. Cabbies receive radio orders on a first call bases, meaning that whenever the dispatcher called out an order, all cabbies in the immediate area would call back their cab numbers and the first cab number the dispatchers hear would be given the order. Cabbies had to stay alert and be quick to respond to orders as they were given out by the dispatcher. However, I would quickly learn that drivers who gave the dispatchers a few dollars, under the table, had their numbers called more often and got the best fares.

Four-thirty in the morning the day after my four hour ride-a-long, I reported for work and was assigned a cab to drive for that day. New cabbies were not allowed to select the cabs they drove. That privilege was given to cabbies with seniority. They, of course, usually chose the newest and most reliable cabs. Most cabbies began their day by cruising Sunset Boulevard in Hollywood picking up prostitutes who were completing their night's work. I had been informed that prostitutes would be able to tell that I was a "rookie" cabbie and they were going to barter the cost of the fare or not pay at all. During my first few days on the job I passed up several people who tried to flag me down because I was too frightened to pick them up. I would only accept fares from the dispatchers. I soon realized I had to find a way to overcome my fear of prostitutes, homeless, addicts, and petty thieves because I was just wasting my time and gas cruising the streets during the early morning hours. Finally, I got the courage to pick up a fare at a twenty-four hour restaurant on the corner of Sunset Boulevard and La Brea Avenue where there were always people hanging out in the well lit parking lot. As I drove into the parking lot, two tall slender black prostitutes dressed in micro miniskirts got into my cab and gave the address of their destination. Immediately, it was obvious that I was a rookie cabbie because I had to ask them for directions. They turned out to be the exact opposite of what I had expected as one of them began a conversation with me. "You new ain't you, honey? How long you been driving?" Even though it was actually my first week, I told her I had been driving about three weeks. I don't know why I said three weeks. Maybe subconsciously I thought it would have garnered me a little more respect. She continued talking, "Honey, you'll have this business down in no time. You just come to where you picked us up every morning about this time and we will just be getting off work. If you don't see us, there are always some of us girls looking for a cab during this time of the morning."

Surprisingly, when we arrived at their apartment they paid me the correct fare and even gave me a tip. Wow, prostitutes weren't as frightening as I thought they were. I headed straight back to Sunset and La Brea and made another pick up. By the time I had dropped off that fare, the regular day customers were calling for rides. Realizing I had achieved a major hurdle as a cabby by successfully picking up and dropping off prostitutes, I was feeling quite proud of myself.

The honeymoon with the prostitutes was short lived. The following morning two prostitutes got out of the cab and paid only half of the fare. When I returned to the office at the end of my shift, I explained to Harold, the supervisor, that there was an eight dollars difference between my log sheet and the cab meter reading because a couple of prostitutes didn't pay their full fare. Harold was an older black gentleman who had driven cabs for thirty years before becoming a supervisor and part-time dispatcher. He wanted to know how I had asked the prostitutes for my money. I attempted to explain by saying, "I told them what the fares…." Before I could complete the sentence, he interrupted me and once again asked me, "How did you ask them for your money?" I didn't understand why he wanted me to give him the exact words but I complied by saying, "Ladies…" Before I could speak another word, he said, "That's where you F…ed up!

You said ladies! They don't know what ladies are. They are bitches and whores. You have to use pimp language on these bitches. You bitches give me my M... F...ing money or I'm going to kick your M... F...ing asses!" I explained that I couldn't do that because I didn't use that kind of language. With a big grin on his face he said, "Son, if you are going to make it in this business, you had better learn yourself a few good curse words."

I finally earned my cabby stripes one rainy morning when a prostitute tossed me a ten dollar bill on a fifteen dollar fare and attempted to get out of the cab. Ironically, I was having a bad morning! The night before, I had an eleven o'clock time slot to do my five minute routine at the Improv Comedy club in Hollywood. Even though time slots usually ran behind schedule, I felt that my chances of getting on stage before midnight were pretty good and there would still be a few people left in the audience. However, anytime nationally known comics stopped by the club they were allowed to go on stage and perform and the comics who were scheduled to perform would have their times pushed back, which meant some comics wouldn't get on before the club closed. My time slot was moved back to twelve forty-five in the morning and by then there were only six people left in the audience. Having not recovered from that experience, I had a "Harold" flashback when she tossed me that ten dollar bill. I don't remember what I said to her but when I finished she had given me another seven dollars and I had taken out all of my frustrations on her for being bumped out of my time slot at the Improv.

After a few weeks of driving, I had mastered the cab business. I learned very quickly that if I maintained a conversation with the customers, I was more likely to get a bigger tip. Since I was a comic, talking was my business of choice. I knew that once I had built the relationships, fares would request me on a regular basis and my clientele would increase. I kept a journal on frequent riders who I was interested in being my regular customers. During our conversations, I was constantly collecting key information that I could use to win them over whenever they rode with me again. If they were entertainment lawyers or agents and they were conversing about some of their clients, when they got out of the cab I would write those names down. I would always find a way to get information on my customers' family members, especially children and grandchildren. Since several people rode in cabs four or five times each day it was just a matter of time before I would pick them up again. My customers would always be impressed when they got into the cab two or three weeks later and I could recall the conversation I had with them about their clients. I remembered their children's names, and school events in which their grandchildren participated. In addition to them becoming my regular customers, they would occasionally increase their financial donations in the form of tips.

Another way some cabbies insured themselves of earning more money was to become a friend of the dispatchers by showing them how much they appreciated their services... The payoff! Dispatchers were not supposed to accept money from cabbies in return for fares but, like the cabbies, they also had families and bills to pay. When a customer called the company for a ride, the dispatchers always asked for their destination. If the fare for the trip was above a certain dollar amount, the dispatcher wouldn't put that call out on the radio where the first cabbie responding would get the fare. The dispatchers would always use predetermined codes to give the good fares to cabbies who tipped them. Since communication from the dispatchers could be heard by all of the cabbies, a "coded call" to my cab may go something like this: "Two thirty-eight are you free?" If I responded "yes", he would say, "Pick up your regular at 1437 North Fairfax." I would know instantly that it was a good fare because I didn't have a regular customer that lived at that address.

Cabbies would have to be discrete when paying off the dispatchers. Some cabbies would go into the bathroom, wash their hands and put the money in a paper towel which they would casually drop into a waste basket near the dispatcher's chair. Other cabbies would buy the dispatcher a hamburger and put the money in the bottom of the bag. I had one of the most unique payoff methods. I would take straws from a McDonald's restaurant and carefully remove the straw from the cover and insert a rolled up five, ten, or twenty dollar bill. After inserting the straw back into the cover, I would walk into the dispatcher's area and while distracting everyone with my daily routine of jokes, I would place the straw in a location where the dispatcher could retrieve it after I had left the office.

My regular customers were individuals from all social and economic levels. However, my most interesting customers were those that I referred to as my "real world" customers, pimps, prostitutes, drug addicts, drug dealers, and people who had been dealt a bad hand of life. One of these customers, Paper Doll, was the oldest of six prostitutes belonging to one pimp. Even though she was in her early thirties, she had managed to hold on to her position as the "Bottom Lady", which in reality meant that she was the top prostitute in her pimp's stable. I learned from Paper Doll, that as within any business, employees are always trying to get promoted. At least a couple of the younger prostitutes wanted her position. Paper Doll pronounced that as long as she could bring home more money than those "Young Thangs", as she referred to them, she wasn't worried about her man demoting her. She said those, "Young Thangs" were still flat-backing but the real money was, "on the take." Flat-backing meant that prostitutes were having sex with the customers and "on the take" meant that they were stealing from them.

I picked up Paper Doll one morning as she ran out of a sleazy motel on the Sunset Boulevard. She asked me to speed away. She had just ripped off an Asian customer for one thousand dollars and she was extremely proud of herself because he was the only customer she had serviced that night. To celebrate her conquest, she asked me to stop at a liquor store so that she could buy a bottle of scotch. When she returned to the cab she gave me the bottle and asked me to take a drink. I thanked her for the offer but informed her that I didn't drink alcohol. She pleaded with me to take a sip because it was good luck to have someone else take the first drink when you are celebrating a rip-off. After considerable thought, I honored her request.

Later that day, Paper Doll called for me to pick her up and when I arrived I was surprised when she said she was going shopping. She was extremely upset when she got into my cab because her pimp had only given her one hundred dollars for her shopping spree. When I inquired about the thousand dollars she had stolen from her customer, she said that she had given the money to her pimp. Being naive, I asked why didn't she take a couple hundred for herself and give him the balance. She said that girls never hold back money from their pimps because they never know when they are going to be stripped searched. She also said, whenever a girl is caught holding out on her man she will be seriously beaten and could end up in the hospital, and in some cases girls had been killed. I enjoyed riding with Paper Doll and listening to her talk because I was getting an education about a lifestyle and a world that I had only heard about and really never expected to see in my lifetime.

Approximately a year after we met, Paper Doll went home to visit her family in Florida. More than three months passed and she had not returned. One morning I saw one of her roommates while I was cruising down the boulevard and I pulled over to inquire about her. Sadly, she said that Paper Doll had died about a month earlier from some bad blow (cocaine) she had taken. I asked if she had met with foul play or had she taken her own life. The roommate assured me that it was just bad blow as several other people had gotten sick and Paper Doll was the only one that had passed away.

I found myself deeply saddened by the news of Paper Doll's death. During the year that I had known her, she had gone from being just another prostitute on the streets to a friend or more like a family member. We had something in common. I was a country boy from Alabama and she was from a small rural town in Florida. Paper Doll had taken me under her wings as her young brother and taught me how to survive driving a cab on the streets of Hollywood. She knew that I had dreams of becoming a comedian and was passing through her world on my journey to my destination. Even Paper Doll had dreams of getting out of the business and she would often share her fantasy about going back home to live with her mother and her eleven year old daughter. There were times when she would throw her head back and have a hearty laugh when she talked about working a day job like real people, coming home, having a big dinner while sitting on the front porch watching cars pass and fighting mosquitoes. Then she would say that she didn't know what type of job she could find because she had been flat-backing since she was sixteen. For a few moments she had laughed and acted as if she was having the time of her life, but all too soon the joyful tone of her laughter would turn to sadness as she appeared to realize that her dreams would never come true. She would often use the phrase, "Real people," as if she was living in a different world or on another planet. Often I engaged in one of my philosophical spiels about all of the possibilities and all the things she could accomplish if she would only set her mind to do them. After patiently listening to my mini sermon, she would reply with her usual response, "Nigger please! Wake up! This is Paper Doll you are talking to!" Even though she was a prostitute, I believe she was one of those angels God had surrounding me.

My favorite pimp, Bernard, was a tall dark-skin soft spoken brother who didn't dress, act or look like a pimp. He usually wore a necktie and occasionally a suit and had the appearance of a college professor. Bernard had five girls in his stable. Even though he was quiet and reserved, it was obvious that he was feared and respected by his girls. I would often take Bernard to the county jail to bail out some of his girls who had been arrested the night before. Bernard explained the business side of prostitution and how local and county governments had an un-written partnership with his industry. He said, "Each time one of my girls is arrested I have to pay three hundred dollars to bail her out of jail and she is back on the street working that night. I have to pay my lawyer three hundred and fifty dollars to make a ten minute court appearance where a judge usually assesses a fine of five hundred to a thousand dollars. Periodically, the judge will sentence a girl to a week in county jail, but he is a part of the system and he knows that the system doesn't make money on locked-up prostitutes. Each one of my girls is arrested on an average of six times a year and there are probably more than three hundred hookers in the city. So when you do the math, the city government is the biggest pimp in town."

I finally got the opportunity to see the 'pimp side' of Bernard one rainy morning as we cruised down Sunset

Boulevard to pick up his girls after their night on the street. Three of the girls rushed to get into the cab as he asked them if they had his money. Two of the three had made their quota and he told the other girl she couldn't come home until she had all of his money. She pleaded, "Daddy, can I come home? I will make it up tonight." Bernard, in an outraged voice said, "Bitch, go get my money! And don't come home until you get it or that's your ass!" As we drove away I was fixated on the young lady with tears rolling down her face, huddled under a small umbrella while Bernard continued our conversation in his mild tone of voice as if nothing had happened. I had become used to other pimps verbally abusing their girls but this was the first time Bernard had raised his voice towards one of his girls in my presence. Most cabbies agree that one of the toughest things about the business is being in the presence of pimps abusing their girls and there is nothing you can do about it.

The most forgotten victims of the prostitution business are the children of the prostitutes. Some prostitutes choose to keep their children rather than give them to relatives or put them up for adoption. These children grow up in a world of drugs, prostitution, and crime. Bobby Mack, a ten year-old chubby white kid with sandy red hair and freckles, lived with his mother in a cheap motel room in East Hollywood. Bobby would roam the boulevard in the early hours of the morning while his mother was servicing her customers in their motel room.

Bobby was well advanced for his tender age and had seen more of the world of prostitution and drugs than I would ever care to imagine. Bobby, along with a few other kids, could be seen throughout the night and early morning hanging out on the streets of Hollywood. I befriended Bobby one morning when his mother paid me to ride him around for about thirty minutes while she "took care of a little more business" as she described it. Bobby was a talkative kid who had been in the streets with his mom for as long as he could remember. He said that he and his mom had lived in Texas before her pimp moved them to California. I asked him if he attended school, a question to which I felt I already knew the answer. Bobby said he had attended a few schools but his mom and her pimp were always moving and he didn't really like school anyway.

Often, when I saw Bobby wandering about the Boulevard before daybreak, I would pick him up and ride him with me for a couple of hours. I would buy him a sandwich and drink for which he was always very appreciative. He talked freely about the business and his hatred for pimps. Bobby said he watched the pimp beat and stab his mother when he was seven years old as he tried to help her. After she came out of the hospital they lived with an aunt until his mom was better and they moved back with her pimp. Bobby passionately talked about killing his mother's pimp in much the same way as the average kid might talk about visiting Disneyland. As he talked, I could feel his pain and knew that unless a drastic positive change occurred in his young life, he was probably going to kill him.

On several occasions, after eating, Bobby would talk himself to sleep. Observing him sleeping I would often wonder what type of life he would have? Would he grow up to be a pimp, thief, murderer, drug dealer, or addict? Would he live a long life, end up in prison or maybe become one of Paper Doll's "Real people?" I tried to figure out why he ended up in my cab and not with some other cabby. What lesson was I learning from him? Could it be possible that he was one of my angels, or was I perhaps one of his angels? After letting Bobby sleep for a couple of hours, I would drop him off on the boulevard. I knew that he would be safe and could find his way home.

Where there is prostitution there is usually a higher rate of crime, violence and drugs. My only knowledge of drugs had been limited to comedians smoking marijuana in the parking lot of the comedy clubs. I often encountered several small time drug dealers and based upon my instincts as a cabby I also had a suspicion if a suspected customer was transporting drugs. One dealer, Larry, gave me a glimpse into the drug world. Larry lived in North Hollywood in a modest home with his wife and two children. On the surface he was a typical white male who could have been a legitimate business man or even a minister. Once a week I picked him up at his home and took him to a storage center in Burbank where he removed a suitcase and a brief case and placed them in the trunk of the cab. I then drove him to the second level of the parking garage at the Los Angeles County Hospital in East Los Angeles where he met a Hispanic gentleman. When I opened the trunk, he took both cases and placed them in the trunk of the gentleman's car. In exchange, the gentleman gave him matching cases which he placed in the trunk of the cab and we drove away. The transaction generally took less than two minutes and I realized the first time I drove him to the parking garage that a drug deal had taken place.

People were always quiet about their personal lives and business when I first began riding them, but once they become comfortable and felt that they could trust me, they talked freely about themselves and their business. Cabbies know all of their regular customers' deep dark secrets because it's human nature to share them with somebody. Talking to cabbies about their businesses and personal lives is safe because the people of their world will probably never cross paths with the cabbies.

Larry later confided in me that he had a sizeable drug market in East Los Angeles which was a predominantly

Hispanic community. He explained that he made his drug exchanges at the hospital because being a white male he would stand out like a sore thumb driving around East Los Angeles. He would draw immediate attention from the police. Also, the local drug dealers and gang members would know that he was probably carrying drugs and that would increase his chances of being robbed.

I often wondered if his neighbors and friends knew of his drug business. He was probably a well respected member of the community, belonged to local organizations and maybe even attended church on Sundays while the users of his product were in the process of destroying their lives.

My favorite Beverly Hills customer was Doctor Westmorland, a surgeon who specialized in treating lung cancer patients. He lived in a large beautiful two-story white house with an electric gate and a black wrought iron fence surrounding his property. He had achieved and surpassed the American Dream by all expectations. However, beneath the surface of what appeared to be his obvious success was a man who was tormented by the very profession that was responsible for that success.

Dr. Westmorland had grown weary of treating and performing surgery on patients who had developed lung cancer as a result of smoking cigarettes. He often vented his frustrations towards the tobacco companies that he believed knowingly added harmful and addictive chemicals to their products that caused tremendous suffering and premature deaths of thousands of peoples around the world. He said, as a young physician he was able, to some extent, to detach himself from the suffering and death of his patients. It was all too easy to rationalize by telling himself, as do many doctors, the patients had made a conscious decision to smoke; therefore, they were partly responsible for their health problems. However, after nearly twenty-five years as a cancer specialist and far too many surgeries and deaths, he found himself having compassion for his patients while realizing that almost all of them really wanted to stop smoking but had become addicted.

Dr. Westmorland believed the Federal Government should be more active in forcing the tobacco companies to produce a less harmful product by reducing the levels of addictive chemicals. Tobacco companies should also be required to give financial support to non-profit organizations and educational institutions that would educate students, beginning in kindergarten on the health hazards of smoking. Also, a set percentage of their profits should be donated for cancer research and patient treatment. He said the real health problem was the tobacco lobbyists who funneled millions of dollars to federal and state politicians to defeat anti-smoking legislation.

Dr. Westmorland's personal issues and concerns were quite different from most of my other customers, but just as real. His frustrations were causing him to feel burned out, consider early retirement, and spend more time vacationing at his summer home in Hawaii. Dr. Westmorland said he was able to escape from the hectic world of pain and suffering by deep sea fishing in the Pacific Ocean near his summer home. I grasped that he was in a "catch twenty-two" situation because his lifestyle and career success was really indirectly connected to the tobacco industry. I often wondered if he had guilty feelings as he lounged in his lovely home and cherished his material possessions. Once again I would wonder whether he too was one of God's angels.

19
ARRIVAL OF FORGIVENESS

Early on September 25, 1983 God blessed me with another angel, my daughter Ania Ayana was born. My wife and I had prepared for her arrival and decided I would become a stay-at-home dad, until Ania was a year old. Comedy was no longer my first priority. It was placed on hold for a few months. My priorities became middle of the night feeding sessions, changing Pampers©, bathing, doctor's visits, and all the responsibilities that came with being a parent. Actually, being a Mr. Mom contributed to my career as I gathered enough comedy material for an album entitled, "The Nightmare of Living With A Pregnant Woman."

My comic friends would frequently express their sympathy for my isolation. I accepted their condolences without telling them I really enjoyed spending time with my little angel. I must confess it was sometimes embarrassing sitting in the doctor's lounge swapping baby stories with a group of mothers. If my buddies had witnessed some of those situations, they probably would have requested my membership card for the, "Real Men's Club."

When Ania was six months old, Brenda's mother moved from New York to relieve me of my "Mr. Mom" duties. I headed back to Los Angeles. God was preparing another blessing delivered by a stranger I would meet in my taxi cab.

July, 1984 I picked up a passenger in West Hollywood and dropped him off at Canadian Airlines at the Los Angeles International Airport. At the time there was nothing special about him and no particular reason to remember him. He was just another person that I transported through the streets of Los Angeles. Exactly, one week later I received a call from the dispatcher to pick up a fare at a West Hollywood hotel. Upon parking my cab, I entered the lobby and to my surprise the gentleman I had dropped off at Canadian Airlines the week before walked downstairs. On impulse, we ran and hugged each other as if we were long lost friends as each of us was caught up in the moment of our one in a million chance of meeting again. On this occasion we introduced ourselves and I learned his name was Edward Mosby. Edward was on his way to a meeting in Brentwood not far from the University of California in Los Angeles. He informed me that the meeting would last approximately an hour and asked if it would be possible for me to return and drive him to Burbank which was about fifteen miles away. Instead of driving back to Hollywood, I decided to wait and read my newspaper while he attended his meeting.

After departing Brentwood and heading to Burbank, Edward asked me what type of entertainer I was trying to become. Being that he was an entertainment lawyer he knew enough about the business to know that most cabbies were actually wannabe entertainers. I proudly informed him that I was a comedian. When he asked me how I was progressing in the business, I replied by saying, "I am going to beat my head against the wall until it falls over." He made a statement that really didn't make any sense to me when he said, "Stop, it will come to you." My question to him was how could you get somewhere without putting forth an effort? He replied,

"Oftentimes when people are trying to get somewhere, they are constantly moving even when they don't know which direction to move in. So, when the opportunity arrives they miss out because they are out of position. Look, you are a nice guy. It will come to you if you'll just stop." Well, that statement prompted me to change the conversation because I saw no logic in what he said and I was thinking to myself that I had picked up a weird white man. We continued our lively conversation until we arrived at the Burbank Studios where I bid farewell to my radical thinking passenger and headed back to Hollywood.

Later that day I picked up a passenger that I dropped off at the Burbank Airport. As a cabbie you really don't want to take a fare to Burbank in the late afternoon because it might take a couple of hours to return to Hollywood due to the heavy rush hour traffic. Furthermore, you would have missed out on most of the regular riders as they got off from work. Needless to say, I was not happy about my trip to Burbank.

Upon returning to Hollywood and while passing the Burbank Studios, I noticed a man with his back to the street talking to a woman. Even though his back was to me, I recognized him by his coat as a fare from the past. Realizing that he had probably called a cab; I decided to make a U-turn and pick him up before the cabby who had received the order saw me take his fare, prompting a possible fight. After he jumped into my cab, I sped back onto the street and in my amazement of bumping into him again, I said, "Hey Edward! Man what a coincidence, picking you up again!" Very calmly he asked, "Why does it have to be a coincidence? Do you think there might be a reason for us meeting like this? There is really no such thing as a coincidence. People only use the word because they don't understand what is really happening." Once again, I began thinking that this guy is really weird and I could write a comedy routine about him. Again, I quickly changed the conversation in an attempt to bring him back to reality. He went on to say how he wanted to go back to the hotel, pick up his bags and be taken to LAX which meant that I was going to get a hefty fare and tip.

After retrieving his bags from the hotel, we were heading down La Cienenga Boulevard towards the airport. We were discussing a news report, which had just aired on the radio, regarding a driver who had lost control of his car and crashed into a group of people waiting in line to see a movie. Unfortunately, a young girl was killed. Once again he made what I thought was another weird and insensitive statement that people who die, want to die; deserve to die; had a premonition about dying or something to that nature. In my mind, he had just stepped on my last nerve and I had taken about all of the "off the cuff" ridiculous statements I was going to take from him. In an effort to shut him up and prove that he was wrong, I unconsciously blurted out that he didn't know what he was talking about because my father had been killed by a white man in Alabama just because I answered his questions with a "yes" and "no" instead of "yes sir" and "no sir." And, he didn't have any premonitions about dying nor did he deserve to die. When I finished screaming at him, he made an even more bazaar statement. "Oh, he didn't kill your father because you said, "yes" and "no." He was going to kill him any way. He just used that moment to do what he was planning to do sooner or later. If you want to be free, all you have to do is forgive the man and get on with your life." Then he made another statement that I felt he had no right to make when he said, "And your father knew he was going to die. He just didn't want to upset you. If you really want to be free, forgive your father for dying and the man who killed him." That statement pushed me over my psychological edge. I asked him if he was crazy, and told him that he didn't have the right to ask me to forgive the man who had killed my father because he wasn't there and he didn't know what had happened. I was so angry I almost stopped the cab to put him out for insulting me with such a ridiculous theory.

From my outburst he could tell it was probably a good idea not to talk to me anymore about that subject. My only concern at that point was to get him to the airport and put him out of my cab. However, after about five minutes of total silence, he rose up on the seat and touched me on my shoulder and said that he was going to make a deal with me. I didn't have to mean it, but if I would just let him hear me say the words that I forgive the man, he would never bother me again. At that point I was so frustrated and angry, I would have said anything just to get him to leave me alone, but I really didn't have any intentions of forgiving anybody for anything. I don't know how I was able to utter the words, but once I said that I forgave Bill, it was as if I had been instantly moved from one planet to another planet. I could no longer feel anger, pain, hatred or any ill feelings toward Bill Carlisle. It was as if Bill Carlisle didn't exist anymore. I was experiencing the most peaceful moment of my life and it was an indescribable high of which no man-made drug could have produced. During the next few miles to the airport, I felt like I was riding above the clouds.

When we arrived at the airport, without me asking, Edward gave me his business card and told me to call him sometime. Upon leaving the airport, I had to find someone to share my unbelievable experience with. I drove directly to visit my friend Brad Sanders, who was also an upcoming comedian. During my sharing of the event, it was obvious to Brad that I had gone through some type of metamorphosis because he had never seen such joy and happiness within me. "Who is this guy?" asked Brad. I replied, "I don't know, just some weird white guy from Canada." As I was walking out of Brad's apartment heading back to work, I said, "Man, forget about that guy. I'm not calling him. If I'm still feeling this way in six months, I might call him."

I actually had forgotten about Edward when approximately six months later I just happened to notice his card on my dresser. A strange feeling came over me at that moment because I had looked at that very same spot on my dresser several times during the past six months and I had not noticed the card. Picking it up, I had a strange feeling as if some kind of spiritual occurrence was flowing throughout my room. The following day, I made the call. The first thing I noticed when he answered the phone was the happiness in his voice as he inquired about how things had been going in my life since the last time he saw me. He seemed genuinely interested about how my taxi and comedy careers were doing as we talked for about thirty minutes on a variety of topics. However, whenever he talked about something that I didn't fully understand, it did not seem as weird to me as it did when we first met. Instead of trying to change the conversation, I eagerly wanted him to continue talking as I tried to understand and even ask questions. I had learned that the habit of closing my mind to things I didn't understand was preventing me from gaining new knowledge that could help me navigate the turbulent waters of life.

Edward and I would continue our phone conversations on a weekly basis for the next several months as I soaked up his invaluable knowledge about life. I was constantly taking notes during our conversations because I wasn't able to grasp and maintain the vast amount of information he was imparting to me. In the spring of 1985, in an effort to really take advantage of his wisdom and knowledge, I flew to Toronto, Canada to visit him. I arrived on a Saturday afternoon where he was waiting at the airport to pick me up. After taking me home to meet his family, they went out on a date with their seven year old twin boys leaving me home alone. Edward had began a tradition with his boys whereby they had two weekends per month when they were allowed to select any event or activity that they wanted to participate in, and that time would be scheduled specifically for them.

Since I was alone, I crawled into bed and took a two hour nap. It was the most peaceful sleep I had experienced since Daddy's death. The main thing that made their home so peaceful was that they did not have a television in the house. Edward said when his boys were four years old he came home from work one afternoon and the boys were in the living room watching television. He spoke to them a couple of times but they were so engrossed in the television show they never realized he was in the room. He proceeded into the kitchen where his wife was preparing dinner and told her that the television had to be removed from the house. Anything that took that much of his sons' attention so that they could not respond to his presence in a room, was not worth having in their house. So the television was replaced with family activities such as reading books, playing games, and spending the weekends going to the movies, ice skating, visiting parks and museums. Nothing, except emergencies, was allowed to interrupt their scheduled family time. It is amazing how much time there appears to be in a day without television. Dinner and conversations are not interrupted by the evening news which is almost always negative. They shared valuable quality time before bedtime.

Edward had arranged his schedule so he would have ample time to spend with me. He provided a crash course for me on the meaning of life, from his prospective. Even though I had forgiven Bill Carlisle, I still was not fully aware of what forgiveness was and how it worked. I learned from Edward that forgiveness is first and foremost about you and not the individual or individuals who mistreated you. Those who mistreated you didn't spend sleepless nights thinking about what they did to you. They are free of you and moving on with their lives. In order for you to be completely free of the pain associated with the incident, you must release them through forgiveness. Forgiveness does not mean that you forget about the individual or incident. It only means that when you think about them you don't become angry or upset. Thus, you have received freedom through forgiveness.

The one thought that lingered in my mind, "Was forgiveness really that simple?" I had flown to Canada expecting to spend hours listening and learning about forgiveness. I was prepared to take notes and be given books that would further detail the meaning of forgiveness. I was expecting to get the connection between religion and forgiveness only to learn that religion really has very little to do with forgiveness. Forgiveness is actually a law of nature and it applies to everyone regardless of race, color, creed or religious beliefs. The atheist who is not able to forgive suffers the same pain as the Christian, Buddhist, Muslim or any other believer. For the first time in my life I felt that I truly understood forgiveness. All the years I spent in the church, I believed forgiveness required a level of spiritual growth which took years to attain. It was a level where you became a qualified Christian, able to forgive like preachers, elders and Prophets. I understood that until you reached a certain spiritual level you wouldn't be able to forgive anyone because God had not yet granted you that ability.

Edward also introduced me to several of his friends who understood the meaning of life in the same way as he did. Their belief was "Life is simple! People make it complicated."

I enjoyed the rest of my visit in Canada. During the day while Edward was attending meetings I used his ten-speed bike to tour the city where I visited the downtown area and rode along the lakefront. After what seemed to be a very short period of time, I was on the plane heading back to Los Angeles. As I observed the formation of the clouds, I recognized the beauty in them as I had never observed before. I felt a connection to the people around me on the plane even though I was not communicating with them and was unable to see the people in front or behind me. I was suddenly a part of this vast universe and not an outsider looking in through some giant glass window and for the first time in years I was excited about life as well as my future.

When I landed in Los Angeles, I hurried to Brad's home to share the highlights of my Canadian visit. Knowing that he was expecting a lengthy dialogue on what I had learned about forgiveness, I delivered my findings in ten minutes. Brad asked, "Is that all?" After further discussion about my trip, Brad also was beginning to understand that forgiveness was not some complicated drawn out procedure that one must go through to achieve peace from one's past horrific incidents and deeds. Brad and I were very close friends who were able to share what was going on in each other's lives as we struggled to move up the comedy success ladder. He was also another one of those angels that God had assigned to keep an eye on me.

The impact of the visit and my understanding of forgiveness would be a gradual process that would dramatically change my life. I now realized that forgiveness works even though I wasn't sure how it worked. The most amazing result was that when I thought about Bill Carlisle, I had no hatred towards him. I couldn't muster even an ounce of anger, and only peaceful feelings surrounded me when I conjured up thoughts of him. I couldn't understand how a man could enter my life, kill my father, and cause such excruciating pain and suffering. I had spent countless hours, for twenty-two years, imagining numerous ways I could inflict all forms of torture upon him. A man, for whom I harbored severe hatred until that afternoon in the taxi, was now just another person who had passed through my life. I was still unable to interpret the true meaning of forgiveness. I rationalized my uneasiness by telling myself that I was having a brief moment of peace, and after a few weeks I would resume my old habits of fighting personal battles with Bill Carlisle. I was convinced my imaginary world of anger, pain, and depression would resume.

20
THE FRUIT OF FORGIVENESS

Approximately one year later without being consciously aware of what occurred, I was performing at colleges and comedy clubs throughout the country. My life was changing and my career in comedy was on the rise just as Edward had predicted. Bill Carlisle no longer played a prominent role in my daily thoughts but was just a fading memory of my past. When I reflect back on how I was able to begin working the comedy circuit, I now realize that God had quietly surrounded me with comedians who freely shared information and introduced me to comedy booking agents and club owners.

My first major opportunity came when I was given an audition to get a paid gig at The Ice House Comedy Club in Pasadena, California. In preparation for the audition I spent two weeks honing my routine at black night clubs in South Central Los Angeles. The great thing about performing before black audiences is if you are not funny, they are not sympathetic like white audiences who tend not to publicly embarrass comedians. However, with black audiences, in addition to boos and snickers, someone from the audience would usually yell out and tell you, "That shit ain't funny! Get your ass off stage!" Every comedian knew that once black audiences validated your act, you were going to do well performing before white audiences. Comics, like me, who did not use profanity in their act, if successful performing before black audiences, were assured of being booked in predominately white comedy clubs.

On the night of my audition, Brad, my biggest supporter, accompanied me to the Ice House in Pasadena. I had performed at the Ice House on several occasions but this was my first audition to determine if I would begin getting paid to perform. Brad and I arrived about an hour before show time and hung out with the other comedians who were also auditioning or were there in support of their comic friends. I was fortunate to be one of three comedians, and the only black, auditioning. Approximately twenty minutes before the show, we met with the club's manager who outlined the program and informed us that we had a maximum of fifteen minutes to show him what we could do. He pointed out a red light in the rear of the room and explained that when that light came on, we had two minutes to wrap up our performance. In keeping with the comedy tradition, comics drew numbers to determine the order in which we would appear on stage. However, there were really no bad spots because the auditions were held in the middle of the comedy show which meant that the audience had been warmed up by other working comedians and were in a good comedy mood.

Prior to going on stage most comedians have a set routine they follow. Some will find a secluded area where they can meditate. Others will prance about the hallways while verbally speaking out their routine and others will medicate themselves with alcohol or drugs. I, however, preferred standing in the back of the club where I could watch the comics on stage and observe the audience reaction. I even had a ritual I performed as I approached the stage. When

I was introduced I would always walk on stage laughing and just before I removed the microphone from the stand I would turn and point off stage to make it appeared as if I had just been in a conversation with someone who said something very funny. Actually, that "stage appearance" had been suggested to me by Edward as a way of immediately capturing the attention of the audience before speaking a single word and getting them interested in what I was about to say.

When my moment arrived, I walked on stage and immediately took command of the audience with my opening line, "Wow, ain't nothing in here but white people! I feel like I just died and went to Utah!" I had acknowledged them with my little race card joke and they showed me their appreciation with hearty laughs and applauses. I took the approach of a boxer working out in the gym and the audience was my punching bag of laughter and I went for the juggler vain. I was totally pleased with my performance and I was sure that I would get hired to perform at the club.

When the club closed, each comic was invited into the manager's office to be given a review of his performance. I chose to let the other comics get their reviews ahead of me and my confidence rose as they came out of the office with big smiles after receiving booking dates. Fortunately Brad, who knew the manager and was a regular paid comedian at the club, accompanied me into the office when it was my turn to get my performance review. I was given a rave review on my performance and was commended on my material being suitable for the club which meant making the white audience comfortable. However, the manager said that he would like for me to showcase again before he made a decision on hiring me. Even though I knew I had a great set and was well deserving of being hired that night, other comics had informed me that most black comics had to audition at least twice regardless of how good their first sets were. I was about to accept another audition date when Brad intervened. On occasions when the negotiations required a slight hostile approach, Brad would revert back into his Chicago street mood which was not always diplomatic but he got his point across. Brad began to rip into the manager by saying, "Oh, come on man, that's bullshit! You saw his show. He killed! He had the audience rolling on the floor. What else you want him to do? He blew away those white boys and you hired them. Don't insult this man like this. You're wrong and you know it." When Brad finished his tirade, the manager nervously agreed and booked me to perform the following month. As Brad would often say, "Sometimes you have to go Ghetto on white folks in order to get them to see the big picture.

21
THE PLAY

Another angel descended into my life in September 1998. I was the guest host at the San Jose Museum of Art when Civil Rights photos on loan from the Smithsonian Museum in Washington D. C. were on display. The display featured 75 black and white photographs by internationally known photographers including Gordon Parks, Robert Sengstacke and Leonard Freed. As host, I gave a brief background about my life growing up during that era prior to visitors touring the museum.

When tours were completed, I stood near the exit and thanked the visitors for coming. One of the visitors, Tommy Fulcher, asked me if I had ever considered performing a play about my life. I replied it had never crossed my mind. He commented that my life story was more interesting than the photos that were on display. After a brief discussion of his idea he gave me his business card and asked me to call him.

When I called Tommy, he asked if I knew anyone who could assist me in writing a play about my life. I told him I knew Ann Johnson who directed plays for Tabia African-American Theatre Ensemble. Tommy instructed me to arrange a meeting at his home with her as soon as possible. I called Ann and told her that Tommy was interested in putting together a production where I would perform a one-man play about my life. Ann asked if I could give her the details about my life that might warrant a one-man play. In addition to telling her about the murder of my father, I gave her a video tape of me speaking at a local church about my life. After viewing the tape Ann asked me if I thought I was emotionally strong enough to perform a play about my life. I explained to her that I had been speaking about my life for the past two years and had overcome the emotional pain of the murder. Ann warned the experience might be very difficult for me because she had to take me back to that afternoon; and she didn't think I had consciously revisited that moment. I assured her it wouldn't be a problem.

When we met with Tommy, he explained his vision and asked how much it would cost to produce the play? Without giving any apparent thought to his question, she blurted out ten thousand dollars. He immediately began to write her a check for that amount and said that he wanted the play completed by January. Ann explained to him that the cost might be greater than the amount she gave him, and the four month time span was too short. She explained we had to conduct research, which included going back to my hometown to locate court records. Tommy responded by saying, "Whatever it cost, I want it done. The only thing I want back is my investment." Later, he declined to accept repayment for his investment.

Ann and I immediately began developing the play. Three weeks later my brother Lindsey and I were in the courthouse in Butler in search of records from the trial. When we approached the courthouse clerk and asked for trial records from 1962, we were directed to the balcony where blacks sat during segregation. The two rows of bench seats had been removed and there were scores of unmarked cardboard boxes with court documents tossed along the floor of the balcony. From the dust and spider webs it was obvious that the boxes had been there for quite some time. Lindsey and I began the task of looking through each of the approximately two hundred boxes, without a clue of where to begin. The boxes were not stored in chronological order. A box with records from 1941 was surrounded by boxes with records from 1939 and 1954.

After a couple of hours toiling through countless boxes, without any success, we went down stairs and explained our dilemma to an elderly, slender, gray haired, black lady sitting at the receptions desk. Her mannerism and the tone of her voice reminded me of my Granny. As she climbed the spiraling stair case, she pulled herself along as she held firmly to the rail. When we reached the balcony she asked what year was the trial held. I told her it was in 1962. After carefully surveying the piles of boxes she pointed to a section in the center of the stack and said, "The records y'all looking for should be in that area."

We were pleasantly surprised when the second box we opened contained the documents from 1962. The third binder I removed from the box was labeled, The State of Alabama vs. William Carlisle in The Circuit Court of Choctaw County, Criminal Division. Inside of the binder was a copy of the Grand Jury indictment of 1st. degree murder filed in the Circuit Court of the State of Alabama, Choctaw County on October 3, 1962. There was a hand written note of the jury's verdict, "We the jury finds the defendant guilty of 1st. degree manslaughter as charged indictment and fix his punishment at nine years in the penitentiary." The note was signed by the Foreman of the jury, Claude Wimberley. A motion to suspend the sentence was filed on October 11, 1963 based upon the financial hardship on his wife, children and elderly parents. A copy of the $5000 bond for Bill's release from jail was posted on November 2, 1962, and was signed by his mother Bernice and mother-in-law Edwina Butts. A motion for a new trial was filed by Defense Attorney, Joe Curl, on November 30, 1963. There were twenty-five reasons listed for a new trial in the motion. Number twenty-three received most of my attention… "For the court erred in refusing to give the following written charge requested by the defendant: The court charges the jury that if you are convinced by the evidence in the case that state's witnesses, Carl Ray and Vidella Ray, swore that Carl Ray hit defendant, William Carlisle, on the head with a bottle one time and that no other person hit the defendant, and if you are further convinced from the evidence that the defendant was struck several times on or about his head, forehead and neck, then you would be justified in reaching the conclusion that said Carl and Vidella Ray swore falsely to a material fact in the case, you would have the right to disregard their testimony entirely and bring in a verdict of not guilty for the defendant." I had gotten so involved in reading the documents the clerk had to come up and remind us that the building would be closing at 5 p. m.

Our next visit was to the local newspaper, "The Choctaw Advocate" to search for newspaper articles that was written about the murder. The editor of the paper was Tommy Campbell, a friendly white gentleman about forty years old. Even though he was only a few years old when Daddy was killed, he said he was familiar with the case. Tommy said the story of what happened to my father had been told to him many times by other whites in the community.

I explained to Tommy the purpose of our visit. I was interested in getting a copy of the paper which contained the article about Daddy's murder. Tommy went into the archives and bought out a paper dated, Thursday, September 13, 1962. On the top right side of the paper was a picture of the yard and house with an arrow pointing to the spot near the shrubs where Daddy's body fell to the ground. Beneath the photo in large bold letters were, "Bond Denied Killer of Elderly Negro."

As I looked at the photo I had a strange feeling that a part of me was still in that picture. I remembered kneeling over Daddy's body crying out to God asking, "Why?" Later I realized that the original person I was actually died that afternoon. I was a completely different person born into the same body. When Daddy took his last breath, which is still vivid in my mind today, the original "me" also took his last breath. I would never again be that happy kid with great academic potentials. I would never sing in another choir, quartet or as a solo act again. I would never be an officer in a church organization or school club. Never!

As I stared at the photo I felt as if I was two different people in one body. The original "me" with whom I identified and the present "me" who I felt I really didn't know. In that moment I began to mourn the loss of the original "me." Before I succumbed to tears I was snapped back into reality when Tommy touched me on my shoulder and ask if I would like for him to make a copy of the article for me. With a copy of the court records and the newspaper article Lindsey and I returned to his home in Montgomery where I spent the night before flying back to California.

When I returned home Ann and I immediately began the writing task. We decided to divide my life into periods with each period being a "scene" within the play. We began with the first five years of my life, and identified each period to be written. The scenes identified were elementary and middle school, high school, the afternoon, Tuskegee Institute, the trial, conversations with Bill Carlisle and forgiveness. Once each scene was written into a stage play format we began rehearsals.

When we began to write the section of the play depicting the murder scene, I realized what Ann meant when she said that she was going to take me back to that afternoon. I had written the scene with me describing the details of what transpired from the moment Bill Carlisle drove into the yard until he drove away. Ann said that she wanted me to play the part of Bill hitting and shooting Daddy. I did not understand why it was necessary to play the role of Bill when I could give the audience a step-by step view of what happened. She explained that the scene would be much more powerful if it was acted out. I was shocked when Ann said, "I'm your father sitting on the porch. I want you to shoot me." I was speechless. Ann began to softly instruct me, "You are Bill. You are getting out of the truck and walking towards the porch. You are focused on this little old black man and his son. Your anger increases with each footstep. You walk up within two feet of them. You pull the gun from your back pocket and strike him on the head. Now you cock your gun and begin to pull the trigger. It's just as clear in your mind as if it was yesterday. Come on, shoot me! Shoot me!"

I was unable to speak or move as every word that she spoke pierced the inner depths of my soul as I was actually reliving every second as it had unfolded that afternoon. I saw clearly the hate filled face of Bill Carlisle and felt the same fear and helplessness I felt as he approached us. I saw the gun as he pulled it out of his back pocket, the crushing blow to Daddy's head, me hitting him with the bottle and I heard the gun shots. During my temporary black out state I was unaware that I fallen to my knees and was sobbing uncontrollably.

After composing myself I told Ann that I couldn't perform the scene. Ann explained that it was the most important scene in the play and without it there could be no play. She suggested that we should practice a portion of the scene each day and when it became too stressful for me we could take a break. The first couple of days were fruitless as I would breakdown just thinking about the scene. The most difficult part was pointing my hand with the imaginary gun in it and pretending to be Bill shooting Daddy. As I looked into that blank space I actually saw Daddy standing there staring back at me. I was in the middle of a nightmare, even though I was awake. The first few attempts I was unable to lift my hand as my body trembled, tears ran down my face and cramps raced up my legs causing temporary paralysis. Almost two weeks would pass before I was able to rehearse the five minute scene and maintain my composure. Even though the scene caused me tremendous anxiety and depression, the therapeutic value was priceless.

Once I was able to rehearse the afternoon scene without losing my composure, we scheduled the première date of the play, July 29, 1999. Ann assembled a group of volunteers to assist us in planning the series of tasks that would be required to bring Tommy's dream to fruition. Ann rented the 2nd Stage Theater located in downtown San Jose and hired a production crew. Norma Callender, Tommy's office manager, was responsible for publicity, programs, tickets, and the reception.

The week before the play I received a call from Casandra Andrews, a reporter with the Mobile Register Newspaper, in Mobile, Alabama. Casandra wanted to talk to me about the play. She said that she was writing a story about a seventeen year old black girl who was killed in Butler during a Civil Rights march in the sixties. Tommy Campbell told her about my story and the one-man play I would be performing within a couple of weeks. Casandra asked if she could do a telephone interview with me the following day at 2 p.m. central standard time. Approximately, an hour later she called back and said she had pitched the story to the editor of the newspaper and he wanted her to fly to California immediately and interview me. Two days later Casandra was in my house in San Jose with a pad and pencil asking questions. After the interview Casandra asked if it would be possible to come see the rehearsal that afternoon so that she could include a review of the play in her article.

Casandra and her photographer sat through the two hour rehearsal as I was directed by Ann and Buddy Butler, Head of the Department of Theater at San Jose State University. Buddy added the three comedy club scenes to the play. Without realizing it, I had written a play that highlighted only the pain in my life. Buddy shared that some people would not be able to absorb the massive amount of pain that I was emitting on stage; and they would walk out. Adding comedy scenes would allow the audience relief from my personal pain.

While Casandra took notes the photographer quietly moved around the room taking pictures. After rehearsal Casandra interviewed Ann and Buddy before rushing off to the airport to board a plane back to Mobile. Her article appeared on the front page of the Sunday Mobile Register Newspaper of which I received several copies.

The excitement of the upcoming production came to an abrupt halt four days before the premiere. I received a call from Fannie, Lindsey's wife, asking me what was going on out there in California. She had read the article and asked why she didn't know about the play. Fannie said that she had called my brother Lemarvin who lived in North Carolina and they decided they should come see the play. Even though Lindsey had gone to Butler with me when I went to the courthouse in search of trial records I never told him I was going to write a play. Without saying what I was really doing, I led him to believe I was doing research for a book.

When Ann arrived for rehearsals on Tuesday afternoon

I informed her that I was not going to perform the play. She became alarmed and wanted to know if I was sick. When I told her because my family was coming, she asked why I didn't want them to come. I just said, "I don't want them here." I broke down and cried like a baby. The thought of them sitting in the audience watching me perform was unbearable. The only thing I could think about was all of the pain and suffering I had caused them by my actions on that fatal afternoon. And I didn't want to re-open those wounds for them. In addition to opening their wounds, four months of rehearsing the play had taken an emotional toll on me. I was concerned that I might not be able to perform in front of them for an hour and thirty minutes.

Ann began pleading with me, telling me I had to do the play because the theater, production crew, and the restaurant had already been paid. Over two hundred guests had RSVP'd and the play was scheduled for Saturday night, just four days away. Ann canceled rehearsal, but insisted the show must go on. During the next two days I would wrestle with one of the biggest decisions of my life. I knew that I couldn't disappoint Tommy because he had invested his hard earned money into the project. Ann had spent countless hours coaching me, holding my hands and supplying tissues during my frequent crying spells. Norma had mailed out invitations to city officials including the Mayor, Police Chief, city council members and other dignitaries. Brad and his wife Joan were flying up from Los Angeles. My mentor from Tuskegee, Mr. Rolan Henry, along with friends from Houston, Denver and Phoenix were coming to see the play.

By Thursday afternoon I knew that I wouldn't be able to live with myself if I disappointed all of my friends, so I decided to do the play. My brothers and sister-in-law, Fannie, were scheduled to arrive on Friday afternoon and stay at our house during their visit. I knew that being around them before the play would have been too traumatic for me, so I checked into a hotel.

After a sleepless Friday night the day that I had feared for four months had arrived. I met Ann at the theater at 3 p.m. for a walk through rehearsal with the sound and light technicians. When I entered the lobby my spirit was up lifted when I saw how Norma had decorated the lobby. There was a huge picture of me on an easel with the name of the theater and the time of the premiere. A red carpet with four stands of pink orchids on each side led to the entrance of the theater. On a table covered with a pink table cloth were programs and a guest sign-in book. An assortment of colored helium filled balloons covered the twenty-foot high ceiling.

After the rehearsal I retreated to the green room where I remained in solitary confinement until the curtains were drawn. I would spend two hours pacing the floor and looking at the clock that appeared to stand still as I grew mentally exhausted and became more nervous with each passing moment. Actually, being nervous was a good sign since some of my best comedy performances came when I was nervous just prior to going on stage.

At exactly 8 p.m. Norma walked on stage and thanked the audience for coming to see the play and acknowledged the dignitaries. When she exited the stage all lights were turned out and I was introduced to the stage via a CD voiceover sound track which was recorded by Brad. "Welcome to the Choctaw Comedy club. Put your hands together for your headliner, comedian Carl Ray."

The moment I walked on stage in the comedy club scene I was in my comfort zone. However, I knew it would only be fifteen minutes before the dreaded afternoon scene and there would be no humor to shield me from the pain I would experience. During rehearsals I was directed by

Ann to mentally take the audience to the murder scene, so for a brief moment they would actually feel as if they were witnessing the murder. However, mentally I should remain outside of the scene so I could continue performing the play. Ann was concerned that the play would come to an abrupt end in the first act if I became overwhelmed and walked off stage, which I had done several times during rehearsals.

With the help of God I managed to survive the afternoon scene. However, the tears and the emotions that the audience witnessed were real. I could see tears running down the faces of people sitting near the stage as I unintentionally transferred my pain into the depths of their souls. During those moments I understood what Buddy meant when he said we needed to add comedy scenes to relieve the pain that some people would feel.

The ninety minute performance was really a therapy session for me and my siblings. For the first time in 38 years I was able to talk to them about what happened to Daddy and how it affected my life. They learned how traumatized I was when I enrolled into Tuskegee less than two weeks after Daddy's death, about the depression, and nervous breakdowns that I experienced during my years at Tuskegee. Being a loner, diagnosed with stomach ulcers when I was twenty years old, and being nurtured by mentors who would not allow me to fail in spite of my mental state. Even though I was talking to them from the stage it began a dialogue which opened up our wounds and began a healing process for each of us.

The performance was emotionally draining. However, when I took my bows I felt as if a huge weight had been lifted off my shoulders. I was instantly re-energized and happily answered questions from the audience for thirty minutes. The reception was a joyous occasion for me and it was the first time since Daddy's death that I truly felt comfortable around my family. I felt like the prodigal son in the Bible, returning home to his family after 38 years in a foreign land. Returning home enabled me to continue the forgiveness process I began in 1984.

22
CURED

Embracing forgiveness had such a positive affect that I began to wonder how much freedom, joy and peace I would experience if I forgave everyone who caused me some kind of pain regardless of how minute. Therefore, I decided to actually search for people and incidents that I needed to release through forgiveness. The first person who came to my mind was Mr. Fowler, a teacher, who slapped me when I was in the third grade. In the early fifties, nurses in medical vans visited schools and vaccinated children against polio. I was extremely afraid of needles and already a polio victim. Therefore, I saw no need to be vaccinated. I was crying and throwing a temper tantrum. Probably out of frustration, Mr. Fowler slapped me. He wasn't being a mean and evil person as I perceived him to be with my young eight-year old mind. But, when I recalled the incident at the age of fifty-five, I was just as angry with him as I was on that day forty-seven years prior. I realized that Mr. Fowler was probably deceased. I did not believe that the incident had any long term emotional impact upon my life, but I felt a great sense of joy and peace by releasing Mr. Fowler through forgiveness.

I began to recall incidents of mistreatment by school-yard bullies. When I was in the fourth grade, I was tripped by a kid name Johnny Anderson as I ran around the school yard playgrounds. While I was lying on the ground crying,

209

Johnny stood over me laughing before running away. When I played that incident back in my mind, it was just as painful as the day that it happened. I honestly had a big laugh as I chastised myself for even remembering the incident. I released Johnny through forgiveness. During the next few months I made a list of incidents, large and small, where someone had caused me pain. I experienced the joy of releasing each one through forgiveness.

In the mist of the excitement of forgiving people, there was one person I never considered forgiving... myself. In 2002 I was watching a minister on television and the title of his sermon was, "What Can You Do When You Can't Forgive Yourself?" That statement drew my immediate attention because I had subconsciously dealt with that question for many years. Self-forgiveness for me was something that was impossible because I had committed an unforgivable deed... caused the murder of my father.

The minister shared a story that was similar to mine. He said he and a friend worked out at a local gym four mornings each week. His friend owned a Rolex watch. He always wanted a Rolex watch but couldn't afford one. One morning his friend rushed off to a meeting and left the watch on a bench in the locker room. He used that opportunity to steal the watch. A short time later his gym bag which had the watch inside was stolen out of his car. Several years later as he began his spiritual journey through life, he was haunted by what he had done. So, he went to his friend and confessed to taking his watch and asked for his forgiveness. He also told his friend that he had enough money to purchase him a new Rolex watch. His friend explained that he didn't have to buy a watch, because it wasn't just any watch it was his father's watch. In fact, his father had given him the watch the morning he passed away.

The minister said he was trapped. The only way to make

his actions right were to go back to that morning and give the watch to his friend. Obviously that was impossible to do, so it was impossible for him to forgive himself. The minister had told my story. I had wished millions of times that I could have gone back to that afternoon and said, "Yes sir" and "no sir." I too was trapped.

In closing his sermon, he said to the audience, "You can forgive yourself, because God has already forgiven you. If God, the creator of everything can forgive you, why can't you forgive yourself? Are you greater than God, yet you can't do for yourself what He has already done? How dare you insult God! Let it go!"

Upon hearing that statement I felt a sense of joy and embarrassment simultaneously. His message arrived at the appointed time. I felt the joy of being able to forgive myself but embarrassed by the possibility that I might have insulted God. However, my joy of was quickly over-ridden by a feeling of guilt. My demons immediately took control and began chastising me for even entertaining thoughts of joy. Thoughts of being unworthy and undeserving rushed to the forefront of my mind. Mentally I was falling back into that bottomless pit of despair. This bottomless pit is often described by people who have suffered from severe depression as the "Dark Place." On several occasions I have heard celebrities who were guests on TV talk shows mention, the "Dark Place" without further explanation. I have only discussed the "Dark Place" with my therapist.

Just as quickly as my demons had captured my mind, God restored it before the minister completed his sermon and gave me a feeling of joy without the guilt. I was basking in the same joy I experienced when I forgave Bill for killing Daddy. I remember thinking that the joy of forgiving Bill was a temporary state of mind and would dissipate in a few days. Thankfully, those ill feelings towards him never resurfaced. Bill could walk into my home right now and I wouldn't get upset. I would probably invite him in and offer him a cup of coffee.

During the next year I really began to feel that I had reached the point of forgiving myself. However, I had questions for God: "Why didn't You send that minister five years after Daddy was killed? Ten years? Or maybe fifteen years? Why did You make me wait forty years when the answer was so simple? Self-forgiveness!" As I waited for God to respond to my questions, the number 40 began to circulate in my head. In the lifetime of Noah, in the Bible, it rained for forty days and nights. The children of Israel were lost in the wilderness for forty years. Throughout the bible the number forty is used numerous times. Maybe through my forty years of suffering I gained some spiritual knowledge or wisdom that I can share with the world. Perhaps my story will release someone from their personal bondage. I once heard the phrase, "You don't have the right to keep your pain to yourself because someone needs to hear about your pain so they can be free." I have often questioned God regarding the years I suffered. Did He allow me to suffer just to have a story to tell? Why did I have to bear that cross? Why didn't He give me a story to share without giving me the pain? It eventually registered that without the tragedy I experienced, I wouldn't have a story to tell. There is also the possibility that if God had sent someone before Edward I might not have been opened to receiving the message. Maybe I just wasn't ready.

Through this journey of forgiveness I was led to a source of pain that I had never consciously addressed. For the first time in my life I began to deal with my feelings regarding my Country, the United States of America. This process was triggered one night after a performance of my one-man play when a white male in the audience asked me if I loved America. I really couldn't answer the question and I felt very uncomfortable standing before the audience searching for words to say. I felt a bit of anger as I tried to maintain my composure while saying, "I have never thought about loving America and I really don't know if a black person could or should really love America." Realizing that I had placed myself into an uncomfortable position with that statement and feeling the silence of the predominantly white audience, I just began to talk while looking for the appropriate words to say. A peace came over me as I began to, for the first time, express how I really felt about America. I began by saying, "I see African Americans as the foster kids of the American family. I worked with foster kids for several years. I often observed that when they reached the age of eighteen and were emancipated from the foster care system, several of them attempted to re-attach themselves to the family members who had rejected them. When they became employed they would share a portion of their meager earnings with their mothers, fathers and relatives. I didn't see that as an expression of their love but instead a gesture of wanting to be accepted into the family. African Americans have fought and died in wars defending the freedom of America and I don't believe it was out of love but the need to be accepted. A way of saying, we are worthy." I had stumbled my way through an awkward situation and the audience appeared to have accepted and understood my little impromptu speech.

During the next several weeks that question continuously seeped back into my conscious mind and I repeatedly repelled it. One night while sitting alone in my hotel room watching a news report about an unarmed black man, who had been shot several times by the police, I was forced to address my feelings. I had to admit to myself that I really didn't like America, the land of my birth. The more I thought about it, the more I disliked America almost to the point of hatred. My first reaction was to admonish myself for having such thoughts which were not God-like or patriotic. Over the next several days hatred towards America kept revisiting my conscious mind. Finally admitting to myself that those feelings had been simmering deep down inside of my soul for many years, I began to ponder how I could deal with them. My first thought was, "forgiveness." I had accepted the fact that I was very angry and America was the major source of that anger and pain. I had forgiven Bill Carlisle for killing Daddy, but in reality all of the blame could not be placed on him. He lived in America where he knew he could kill any black person and not be justly charged or held accountable. So, America shared just as much guilt as Bill Carlisle in the murder of my father. In order for me to be totally free of hatred, I knew I had to relent and forgive America.

Once again, with a pad and pen in hand I began to make a list of my grievances against America. I recalled that on June 10, 1963, nine months after Daddy was killed, I was locked in a hotel room in Meridian, Mississippi and harassed by eight Klan members. I harbored anger towards them for years, while my subconscious anger toward America grew. America didn't have a justice system for black citizens. Therefore, the law did not punish white people for their criminal deeds. My list grew as I recalled the history of the black man in America: with slavery, the Jim Crow Era, the lynching of almost five thousand black Americans, the murder of Emmitt Till, the bombing of the 16th Street Baptist Church in Birmingham, the assassination of Megar Evers, the murders of James Chaney, Andrew Goodman, Michael Schwerner, dozens of murdered Civil Rights Activists, and thousands of black males railroaded into America's prisons. If the thousands of individuals who committed horrible crimes against black Americans had been brought to justice and punished, maybe, I could love America.

I was now faced with the greatest challenge of my life... forgiving America. I remembered Edward's philosophy, "Forgiveness is not about those who have mistreated you. Forgiveness is about your freedom." Even though that philosophy had helped me to forgive Bill Carlisle, I still wasn't sure if I could forgive America. I recruited my therapist to assist me in the forgiveness process. I realized I had far more anger and hatred towards America than I could ever have harbored against Bill Carlisle. My therapist suggested that in forgiving America, I should also forgive those individuals who caused my actual pain because they were in a partnership. The group that immediately came to my mind was the, "Police." In fact, my deep dark secret which I had not shared with anyone was my enormous hatred for policemen. A few days prior to going to therapy I confided in Brad my feelings towards policemen and he kind of flipped it off by saying, "Yeah, you hate police. Who doesn't?" Then I told him that my hatred for policemen was so strong I hated myself for harboring such hatred. I said, "When I hear about a policeman getting killed, the first thought that enters my mind is, Good! Kill them all!" Then I beat myself up for having those thoughts which I couldn't discuss with anyone." After hearing that statement, Brad appeared stunned as he told me I had a serious problem and maybe I did need help.

During therapy I was able to discuss and examine my negative feelings although I really knew where the source of my problem came from. It was a culmination of all the police brutality against black Americans I had witnessed while growing up in Alabama and Mississippi. My greatest source of pain was vented at the Los Angeles Police who constantly terrorized me during the years I lived there. Prior to moving to Los Angeles, I lived in Silicon Valley. I had never been harassed by the police and had only received one traffic ticket in my life.

When I arrived in Los Angeles, I would often hear my friends discussing how they were being harassed and mistreated by policemen and it all sounded so foreign to me. Then one night, I was stopped by the police for allegedly running a red light even though I was positive that the light was green when I entered the intersection. I was standing near the front of my car with one officer while the other officer sat in the patrol car writing the ticket. I told the officer standing with me, that no way did I run that red light. The officer finally said, "Yeah, I know you didn't. Listen, go downtown pay the twenty-eight dollars for the ticket and ask for a court date. When you go to court for the hearing, he will not show up and the court will dismiss the ticket and refund your money." I followed the advice of the officer and sure enough, his partner didn't come to court and a couple of weeks later, I received a refund check in the mail. Armed with that information, each time I received traffic tickets, I would go downtown, pay the tickets and request a court date. Fortunately for me, none of the officers came to court and I was refunded my money each time.

I noticed as I sat in the courtroom that the overwhelming majority of the defendants were black and Hispanic and all of the judges were white. Observing the scowls on their faces and the tone of their voices it was obvious that those judges had no love or respect for the defendants in their court. In every case where the police officer appeared in court to defend his reason for issuing a ticket, the judge ruled in favor of the officer and charged the defendant the maximum of fifty-four dollars. By charging the maximum penalty, the judges were sending a powerful message that the defendants would have been better off paying the twenty-eight dollars and not wasting the court's time. Observing those kangaroo court judges being so mean spirited and evil further increased my anger towards America. Even though I was blessed that none of the officers who had written me a ticket appeared in court, I still harbored the anger of being issued tickets for violations I had not committed and having to take days off work to go to court to defend myself.

I had the opportunity to see how whites were treated when I received a ticket in Beverly Hills. I followed the same routine as when I received a ticket in Los Angeles. The first thing I observed as I entered the Beverly Hills courtroom was, I was the only black person. When the judge entered the courtroom he politely said, "Good morning. How are you all doing?" The Judge's attitude was a stark difference from the attitude of the judges in downtown Los Angeles. The first person to have her case heard was a middle-aged white woman. While attempting to explain her case the judge tossed her ticket aside and told her to go out and spend some money. There were chuckles from the audience as well as the officer who issued the ticket. The next case was for a young white male who had received four tickets. The judge fined him seven dollars each for two tickets and dismissed the others. The young man objected to having to pay for two of the tickets because they would go against his driving record. The judge appealed to the audience by saying, "Am I a fair judge? I could charge him fifty-four dollars for each of the four tickets. I am charging him the minimum of seven dollars each for two tickets and I threw two tickets out. Is that not justice?" The audience unanimously cheered their approval of the judge's decision. When my case was called, the judge told me to raise my right hand and asked, "Do you promise to give up this violent life of crime that you are leading?" I said, "Yes Your Honor." He replied, "You are free to go." The courtroom atmosphere was more closely related to a comedy talk show than a court of law. While leaving the courtroom, it dawned upon me that I was in Beverly Hills where whites who could probably afford to pay were having their tickets dismissed and were told to go out and spend some money. Yet, just twenty miles away in downtown Los Angeles, poor blacks and Hispanics were being charged the maximum penalty for a similar traffic violation and my anger grew. The victim and witness of hundreds of random black males pulled over by policemen, cars searched and released was infuriating.

My path to forgiving policemen led through some thought provoking questions and statements made by my therapist. "You are torturing yourself with hateful thoughts about police. Everything is being played out in your head. Therefore, you have a choice of getting upset when you see or hear comments about a policeman or the choice of not getting upset. You have forgiven the man who killed your father. Do you think you could forgive a few policemen who have committed far less harmful acts against you?" I finally had to accept the fact that my anger was not an antidote for their prejudice and racism, but a cancer to my mental and physical health. Her rationale opened a window in my mind and suddenly I could see above the pain and anger that had festered towards policemen.

I would venture to say a large percentage of African Americans have never contemplated how they actually feel about America, and definitely have not entertained the thought of forgiving America.

As I reflect back over the numerous valleys and peaks in my life, I often wonder what the journey might have been if I had known the secret of forgiveness five years or ten years after Daddy's death. What path would I have chosen that could have launched my life in a different direction?

Forgiveness has led me to understand why I made the

radical choice to change careers. My friends and some family members were baffled when I abruptly left my job, sold my house, and moved to Hollywood. Actually, I really didn't have any logical answers for many of the choices I made during that period of my life. I now understand that God had set the stage for me to meet a stranger in a taxi who would free me from my self-imposed bondage and save my life. God knew the guilt and shame that I carried deep down in my soul that I was not going to share with anyone. He also knew that demons were slowly destroying my life through self-hatred and self-sabotage. God used comedy as a medication for my emotional and physical illness. I had to accept the ageless proverb, "God may not come when you want him, but He is always on time."

He kept me alive until I discovered the cure in The Power of Forgiveness. Forgiveness of classmates, forgiveness of family, forgiveness of the KKK, forgiveness of self, forgiveness of a murderer, forgiveness of bigots, forgiveness of the justice system, and forgiveness of American racism freed me. My Advice: Forgive and live. **Accept the cure**!